COMEDY EXPLOSION

A NEW GENERATION

photos: **ED EDAHL**   *text:* **HANK GALLO**

THUNDER'S MOUTH PRESS

NEW YORK

Published by
Thunder's Mouth Press
54 Greene Street, Suite 4S
New York, NY 10013

Library of Congress Cataloging-in-Publication Data

Edahl, Ed
    Comedy explosion : a new generation / photos by Ed Edahl ; text by
Hank Gallo ; foreword by Robert Klein. — 1st ed.
        p.   cm.
    ISBN 1-56025-017-8
    1. Comedians—United States—Biography.   I. Gallo, Hank.
II. Title.
PN2285.E33 1991
792.7'028'092273—dc20   91-23999
                                                                     CIP

Text design by Louey/Rubino Design Group

Printed in the United States of America

Distributed by
Publishers Group West
4065 Hollis Street
Emeryville, CA 94608
(800) 365-3453

Contents

To Janet who pointed Ed's camera in the right direction and to everybody that Hank ever laughed with or at.

Special thanks to Cara Benson, Kimberly Blake, Sandy Brokaw, Richard Fields, Jan Frazier, Bill Grundfest, Caroline Hirsch, Cary & Suzanne Hoffman, Lucien Hold, Michelle Marx, Kate McMahon, Claudia Menza, Campbell McClaren, Michael O'Brien, Peggy Reed, Glen Schwartz, Susan Toepfer, the comics in the book and the waitresses at the clubs (Joy and Jennifer please take note).

An Element of Danger

Meryl Streep, the gifted American actress, once asked me: "How do you do it?" It is primarily actors and actresses who are most in awe of stand-up comedians, especially stage actors who have performed before live audiences. They knew well the sense of immediacy, the "nowness" of the live context. No technological facsimile here. No chance to cover the imperfections and mistakes. No "take-twos." Plenty of creative angst and, at times, downright terror in anticipation of facing the paying throngs. But any actor will tell you that at least he has the comfort of the ensemble with whom he exchanges lines on stage; the stand-up comedian must face the crowd entirely alone—akin to a bullfighter. Even a bullfighter has picadors who torment and weaken the creature with long spears before the bullfighter goes in for the kill with his sword. The comedian has no such weapons. His sword is his wit—manifested in the word, the gesture, the facial nuance. He has no picadors, although the idea is appealing. It would be useful to the comedian sometimes to have several assistants with long spears (with harmless Nerf ends of course) poking the audience into life, bigger laughs, and general realization that this stuff is funny. On tough nights it would be useful to remove the Nerf ends and use razor-sharp spears instead. But just as in bullfighting, there is an element of danger in the mission of the stand-up comedian. Try it sometime, and you will most assuredly agree. The seeming brazenness of an individual who stands "in one" before an audience in order to make them laugh makes the stakes very high. Failure in such a situation is apparent to one and all—painful and humiliating, impossible to hide. The nobility of the bullfighter's quest is open to question, depending on one's taste and cultural background. In my view, however, making people laugh is a very high calling indeed. The late Norman Cousins claimed that the palliative effect of comedy saved his life during a near-fatal illness. Could this be true? Ironically, I wanted to be a doctor when I entered college but a few things got in my way: namely, calculus, physics, chemistry, biology, zoology, organic chemistry, reading, spelling, aptitude, attitude, inclination, attendance, and talent. Naturally, I majored in history and political science, the proper preparation for comedy. We have hardly begun to calculate the benefits of laughter, but we know it makes us feel better. It would surely be a harder life without our collective sense of humor. In fact, it is safe to say that life without laughter would hardly be worth living. Fortunately the world is full of talented comedians, most of them amateur, many of them brilliant, who make us laugh at work, at family gatherings, and on social occasions. They make our lot easier, they enrich our lives. But with all due respect to the amateur and the dilettante, it is a quantum leap from performing for your friends at a party to the challenge of being funny in a professional context. Unlike "that funny guy at work," the stand-up comedian must perform on demand, for remuneration, at a time and place of someone else's choosing—by any stretch of the imagination a formidable task. The subjects of this book are true warriors: complex and intelligent, vulnerable and perceptive, with all the courage of even, yes, a bullfighter.

—Robert Klein
March 1991

v

Caroline's and the Comedy Room

Recently, I was looking through my old files and photographs from the beginning of Caroline's. I realized how much comedy had changed when I came across a photo from the mid-'80s: It was of Gilbert Gottfried and his hair was in a quasi-afro. Then I started thinking about how much even Caroline's had changed since the club went all-comedy in 1982. Not only have we grown right along with the industry, we've actually helped make this business of laughing boom.

Headlining comics was, in itself, a pretty revolutionary idea at the time. Otherwise, only showcase clubs were featuring comedy. We gave our acts an hour a night for six nights out of the week so that they had a serious outlet for their material. And, not only were they sustaining the audiences' attention for the hour, they were killing. We knew we were onto something. But we also knew we needed to get the word out about this new phenomenon emerging from our small room in Chelsea, and I hounded the newspapers about sending reviewers down to the club. Finally, we got Hank Gallo to feature us in the *New York Daily News* entertainment section. Then, comedy's piece of that section got a little bigger. And a little bigger. Until finally, Hank got his own weekly column devoted entirely to comedy. Stephen Holden of the *New York Times* began doing half-page stories on the "new breed of stand-ups" and regularly reviewed our comics as well.

As the reviews got bigger and better, so did our audiences. Casting agents were scouting nightly, and producers and record company execs and cable company programmers were all crowding our room, trying to get in on the development of this "rock and roll of the '80s." The HBO folks and the "Late Night with David Letterman" gang were especially interested, and it got to the point that one night on the air Letterman called our club a subsidiary of NBC because we were getting so many plugs.

Comedy was definitely becoming a major factor in cable programming, and all of the cable channels started to get in on it. We had Showtime shoots and MTV crews in all the time. It became obvious that we needed a bigger room; the demand was there. So in 1987, we moved downtown to larger quarters in the South Street Seaport and designed the new club to be cable-ready. Now any cable TV crew could literally plug into the back of the building and send a feed directly to their trucks. We decided that if we were going to have a shoot almost every other week, we might as well make our room double as a studio.

Taping became so easy, and we became so well-known for spotting good talent, that A&E asked us to do a show of our own.

That was in 1989, and obviously, the boom had become an explosion.

It's 1991, and we are moving to yet another, bigger space. We're now producing shows not only for A&E, but also for Comedy TV, the 24-hour-a-day all-comedy network (who knew?), and various other outlets.

So, the jokes are on us. Really.

—Caroline Hirsch
Caroline's
New York, 1991

Introduction

The national debt was spiraling to the multi-trillion-dollar mark, the streets were awash with drugs and dealers, homelessness was reaching painfully alarming rates, and government officials were paying more attention—and much more cash—to missile production than to medical research. Suddenly, as the Me Decade of the '70s grudgingly gave way to the Greed Decade of the '80s, something odd happened in this country: the comedy scene experienced an unbelievable boom. Then again, perhaps it really wasn't all that strange. When you think about it, we were obviously aching for a few good laughs.

And we were able to get 'em wherever we wanted 'em. If, as they say, laughter is the best medicine, Americans had no problem filling their chuckle prescriptions. While sitcoms like "Family Ties" and "Cheers" helped keep people at home, big screen comedies like *Back to the Future* and *Moonstruck* brought them back out. And since we were going to be out anyway, why not make a night of it —why not see someone live?

The timing for that urge could not have been better, for the comedy club scene was ready to grow. In the '70s there were only a handful of notable showcase clubs on either coast and just a few more in the middle of the country. But by 1983, according to Barry Weintraub, publisher of the stand-up industry publication *Comedy USA Newswire,* there were some 50 to 75 full-time, bona fide comedy clubs in the nation—a number that grew to 200 by 1985 and increased to more than 300 by the end of the decade. In short, stand-up comedy, once show business's poorest relation, was quickly becoming a force to be reckoned with.

Much of this has to do with simple economics; after all, most of the time providing a showcase for stand-up is a relatively inexpensive enterprise. Unlike music clubs, which usually require somewhat sophisticated sound systems, all you need to open a comedy club are the bare essentials: four walls, a stage, a mike, and in most states, a liquor license. As Richard Jeni pointed out in a 1989 *Rave* magazine interview, "It's extremely cheap to put up a comedy club—all you need are a few satin baseball jackets and 15 or 20,000 eight-by-ten glossies of unknown comedians that are used to construct the walls."

Of course, Richard has left out what remains the most important ingredient in any such venture— the actual comic. Now, while some of these people make a nice chunk of change on the road (make no mistake about that), comedians are, as a rule, a rather low maintenance lot. Let's face it, if someone's hungry enough, they'll work for scraps. But even the highest-priced comics (most of them, anyway) arrive for work with few extra demands on club owners; there are no roadies to feed and house, no entourage to cater to, and best of all, no temperamental drummers to bail out of jail shortly before show time.

It was like a show-biz dream come true: something that was cheap and—God love it—popular. None of this has been lost on Hollywood, a town that can spot a trend as soon as it can't ignore it any longer. If the public wants comedy, the West Coast sages figured, let's get us some comics. What a concept!

In addition to other comedians-turned-big- and small-screen stars, Bill Cosby and Roseanne Barr became the reigning king and queen of prime-time television; David Letterman and Arsenio Hall started drawing impressive, demographically correct audiences to the late-night talk show arena; and the likes of Pee-wee Herman (*Pee-wee's Big Adventure*), Michael Keaton (Batman), Steve Martin (*All of Me*), and Eddie Murphy (*Coming to America*) all did downright stand-up business at the box office.

Cable, too, answered the comedy call. Among other specials, HBO brought us Robin Williams "Live at the Met" and Billy Crystal's performance at the Pushkin Theater in Moscow. Showtime, in the meantime, had Elayne Boosler throwing a landlocked "Party for One" and Carol Leifer in the middle of the ocean starring in her own "Comedy Cruise." It didn't end there—there were the "One Night Stands" and the "Young Comedian Specials" on HBO and the "Comedy Club All-Stars" outing on Showtime.

Even basic cable got into the act. To name only a handful, Mario Joyner hosted MTV's "Half-Hour Comedy Hour," Rosie O'Donnell did the honors for VH-1's "Stand Up Spotlight," and A&E bookended the country by bringing us "Live at the Improv" from Los Angeles and "Caroline's Comedy Hour" from New York. But even that didn't seem like enough to laugh about, so in 1989 HBO launched a 24-hour basic service, The Comedy Channel, and in 1990, MTV followed that with HA! The TV Comedy Network. Neither channel, to be sure, exactly set the world on fire but execs at both outfits still thought enough about the idea to merge the two in 1991. Despite Paul Provenza's joking campaign to call the new channel "Shemp-Vision" (in honor of his favorite Stooge), it was rechristened Comedy Central when it debuted in July 1991.

With all of that, one might think comedy was headed for overexposure. Instead, we started buying comedy albums by Emo Philips, Judy Tenuta, Steven Wright, and even Weird Al Yankovic (don't deny it now—he couldn't have bought them all himself). And as if that weren't enough, tens of thousands of us actually flocked to sporting arenas—arenas!—to see such shocking comics as Eddie Murphy, Sam Kinison, and Andrew Dice Clay try to turn every seat in those places blue.

Hell, even Canada jumped on the new chuckle wagon. Our northern neighbor's annual Just For Laughs Festival has been turning Montreal into a virtual two-week-long comedy camp every July since 1982. In fact, in the relatively short time since it began it has become the largest international festival of its kind. Okay, so it remains the only international festival of its kind, but you definitely get the point.

If somehow you don't, however, what can we say? Lighten up! After all, it's as obvious as the phony glasses and bulbous plastic noses on your faces that stand-up comics have definitely started to get plenty of respect in the last decade-and-a-half, no matter what Rodney Dangerfield happens to think.

—H.G.
1991

Judy Tenuta is a gum-chewing, accordi-on-toting, self-proclaimed petite-flower/giver/goddess/buffer-of-foreheads/fash-ion-plate/saint who demands adora-tion. So much in fact, that she insists that her fans convert to "Judyism." But seeing as she is a relatively benign goddess, she keeps the conversion process rather uncomplicated. Her audiences must simply stand up and repeat the following: "I promise to destroy all pigs who do not worship Judy. I will smash them. I will kill them. I will maim them. And then I will date them."

Exercising (exorcising?) this ritual, she claims, allows her devotees to "forget about their prob-lems for a little while and think about mine for a change." You see? Tenuta really is a giver. Just ask her. She'll tell you.

Not like those takers—those countless toads out there: like her hefty former roommate Blosanne ("I hate to talk behind her back, but it's safer that way"); or those smarmy leisure-suited guys who always try to pick her up ("I was looking for some-thing a little higher on the food chain," she often tells them); or, even John Lennon's widow, Yoko Ono ("I'm sorry," she asserts, "but if that guy had aimed a little to the left, he'd be a hero today").

Yep, she's a giver through and through. Only a giver, after all, would bother to ask audience members if they have ever gone on a date with someone "just because you were too lazy to commit suicide?"

Still, she feels not everyone appreciates the goddess as much as they should. Take, for in-stance, the neighbors who frowned upon her di-vine attitude while she was growin up in Oak Park, Illinois, (the same birthplace, she points out, of Frank Lloyd Wright and Ernest Heming-way that accounts for her propensity to "sit in un-comfortable chairs and shoot moose"). Or her classmates at "St. Obnoxious in Bondage, an all-girls punk rock high school, "whom she refers to as "pigs." Or the equally unfriendly college co-eds who wouldn't let her into a sorority be-cause "I already had a personality of my own." And, most sadly, even the people she calls Mom and Dad fall into this rather unflattering category.

"My parents have no concept of what I do. They'll say, 'Oh, Judy, we love you' and then they'll go watch the Cubs game or something." Like everyone else," she sneers, "my parents say they like me but they're liars. They're takers, that's all, takers! I'm a giver and they're takers!"

Still, there are those who hold an undying pas-sion for her—like the legion of "stud puppets," who, she says, are anxious to fulfill her every god-dess-wish. Granted, every now and then a weirdo slips in (like the guy who asked her to bless a photo of his pet poodle), but by and large her devotees are just "normal, everyday love slaves."

judy tenuta

But when she tires of the masses, she can al-ways turn to fellow comic Emo Philips who presented her with a heart-shaped ruby and diamond ring in 1989. And even though she had been known to wear it on her left hand at the time, she coyly main-tained that it wasn't an engagement ring—merely a gift from a pal.

"Emo gave me this," she said then, holding the ring up to the light, "and in return I gave him a nice big box of Huggies—so don't tell me that wasn't an equal trade-off."

In truth, however, as New York radio deejay Howard Stern disclosed in early 1991, it was actually a wedding ring. Judy and Emo, he an-nounced shortly after getting hold of a copy of their marriage certificate, had been secretly hitched in a civil ceremony at New York's City Hall in 1989.

The couple, it should be pointed out, who made a secret of their dating relationship for years, have never denied the report. Still, both

have kept mum on the topic. Which is okay by us if that's the way they want it. After all, who are we to argue with a giver-goddess and her man?

JUDY ON. . . .

The simple things in life: I like to watch a child play on a swing or see a Hare Krishna get French-kissed by a jackhammer.

The man in her life: I'm dating the Pope. Actually, I'm just using him to get to God.

Creative financing: They got mad at me at my college just because I used my student loan to buy a Corvette.

'Friends are just enemies that don't have the guts to kill you.'

Squashed dreams: I majored in nursing but I had to drop it because I ran out of milk.

Responsible behavior: We cannot go around shooting others just because they have no reason to live. If we did, there would be no accountants.

Schoolwork: I got an A in philosophy because I proved my professor didn't exist.

Civil service employees: They have a philosophy course that prepares you for the Post Office. It's called 'I Think, Therefore I Am Over-Qualified.'

Her mommie, dearest: My mother told me, 'Judy, you'll never amount to anything because you always procrastinate.' I said, 'Oh, yeah? Just wait!'

Interpersonal relationships: Friends are just enemies that don't have the guts to kill you.

Richard Belzer's comedy is best compared to jazz. For starters, it's at its most electrifying when it's live, when he's just scatting with the audience. And while there is some structure to his act (make no mistake about that) he's capable of going off on any tangent imaginable—or more specifically, unimaginable. At the taping of his 1986 HBO special, for example, he segued from a riff about "why gay midgets can't find housing" to one about why kids are so confused ("If they like Rambo and Bruce Springsteen, what do they do? Blow up their girlfriend's house and then write a song about it?") and, eventually, he even introduced a little musical called "Jazz for Jesus" ("What a cat! What a dude!").

Also, like jazz, Belzer is something of an acquired taste. At least, it seemed that way when he was starting out at showcase clubs like New York's Catch a Rising Star. Maybe the room wasn't always full in those days, but he did become something of a cult figure. While, as we all know, there is no money in comedy cults, he did earn a certain cachet as established stand-ups like George Carlin, Richard Pryor, and John Belushi made their way to see him. At the time, he jokingly referred to himself as the "pet comic to the stars."

In truth, he was only half-joking. Famous people just kept following him around. One memorable night in 1986, for instance, Robert De Niro, Al Pacino, Christopher Walken, and Daryl Hall shared a table for his show at Caroline's.

"For a while," he says, "I was just known as a New York hipster and all these famous people would come and see me. But I had no money. Now I have a little money and the famous people still come to see me, and so does the general public."

So what kept the average Joes and Janes from finding this guy? Probably fear. He could be so

richard belzer

merciless on stage that Robin Williams once described him as "the Marquis de Sade as a game show host," and David Steinberg, in a *New York Daily News Magazine* story, opined that Belzer was "the comedy equivalent of Mick Jagger—he's threatening and spontaneous."

Much the same can be said for Belzer's life. He grew up in Bridgeport, Connecticut, a battered child whose mother "was like Joan Crawford on acid." Rebellious from the start, Belzer was expelled "from every school I ever went to."

"God," he jokes, "expelled me from Hebrew school—personally. Now I'm officially a Christian."

That pattern held straight through college and after even being thrown out of that, he enlisted in the Army. Following his discharge, he dabbled at jobs as a census taker, a jewelry salesman, and a journalist. Then, in 1971, with no prior performance experience, he auditioned for the underground movie, *The Groove Tube*, and got a part.

It was the beginning of what has proven to be a roller-coaster career. There were the ups (roles in *Fame* and *Scarface*) and the downs (drug use and a bout with cancer), but the thrice-married Belzer took it all as it came.

"I think careers are cumulative things," he says. "A bunch of things add up and after a while you realize you're in a certain position you weren't in five years ago."

See? Exactly like jazz. Sometimes you don't know where it's all going.

RICHARD ON. . . .

Check-ups: Doctors get real personal, don't they? Let me educate the women a little bit. When men go to the doctor, we don't put our feet in stirrups. They don't play country and western music. It's a whole different thing.

For some reason when a man goes, the doctor grabs a man by the balls and says, 'Cough.' I want to know why. What's he looking for? 'Oh,

you've got night blindness, huh? What, you got tennis elbow? Trick knee?'

'Doc, get your hands off my balls!'

I love when doctors have the audacity to put a plastic glove on and grease up their finger. I go, 'Whoa-oa-oa! Doc, I'm paying for the visit right? Well, here's twenty extra bucks, stay out of my ass! Here you go—and unless you're going to wash dishes, take the glove off now!'

Modern cartoons: When I was a kid, the worst thing that happened was Mickey Mouse lost a shoe! What a tragedy! Now, it's a guy in the basement who threatens to eat your family and says, 'I'm gonna put a chainsaw up your ass!'

'God expelled me from Hebrew school—personally. Now I'm officially a Christian.'

I n 1986 Marsha Warfield came by her most successful TV role—Roz Russell on "Night Court"—the hard way. The *real* hard way. The two women who had previously filled the shoes of the show's bailiff, Selma Diamond and Florence Halop, passed away from cancer in two consecutive seasons. And since the role seemed like a killer, wasn't Warfield worried about following in their footsteps?

"I always found that to be a really bizarre question," she says. "It's like asking if I was afraid that I would all of a sudden become an older white woman."

Bizarre or otherwise, Marsha did, however, always find humor in the topic. When asked the same question on "The Tonight Show" around the time that she first got the job, she answered: "Hey, it doesn't bother me. It's sort of like becoming the Queen—it was the only way to get the job."

Sounds logical enough—but well more than a decade of trailblazing stand-up experience under her belt certainly didn't hurt either. Warfield, who was born on the South Side in Chicago, started working for the phone company right out of high school. There the eighteen-year-old met and married the boss's son. In no time at all they realized that this was a very wrong number and the two quickly divorced. They had no children, and Warfield, who jokes that kids "are like husbands—they're fine as long as they're someone else's," has never walked down the aisle again.

After that episode Warfield left the phone company—but stayed in communications. She began performing stand-up comedy in her hometown in the early '70s, when a black female comic was definitely a rare thing. That she did it with an act that was as tough as her neighborhood, however, made her rarer still.

While agents and critics tried to get her to tone down her on-stage patter, Warfield held

steady. And by the mid-'70s she was making a name for herself in Los Angeles. In 1979 she hit a career milestone when she won San Francisco's International Stand-Up Comedy Competition (even besting Harry Anderson, the man who would become her "Night Court" judge).

Despite what some of her critics have said, Warfield has never seen her act as something terribly blue. "When I started doing comedy," she says, "women saying four-letter words was something that didn't happen too often. But nowadays, a woman doing the same act wouldn't get the same label. Let's just say the times have changed, but the label, for me, has hung on."

And over the years, some audience members haven't always hung out to the end of her show. (Marsha once told a well-dressed "Comic Relief" audience that that benefit was akin to throwing a big birthday party but not inviting the guest of honor.) "Sure," she says, "people have walked out every now and then, but nobody ever left in droves. And I always welcome people to leave rather than to sit there and ruin the show for everyone else. I'll even pay them to leave. I'll pay for their cover and their drinks.

marsha warfield

"Once," she recalls with a laugh, "I offered somebody my car keys. In fact, I offered him anybody's car keys. I told him, 'Nobody wants you here.'"

MARSHA ON. . . .

Anatomy: Penises are fascinating. . . . Why do men name them? 'Oh, I see Bob is awake.' Women don't do that. You'll never hear a woman say, 'I'm sitting on Margaret.'

Mr. Right: The good thing about dating younger men is that even if they might not be able to do it well, they can do it more often. I can teach them the rest. . . . Some people tell you that old men have more endurance—they can do it longer. Let's think about that. Who wants to fuck an old man for a long time?

Very young lovers: I told my paper boy, 'From now on I want my paper delivered inside the house. Don't argue with me, I have cookies.'

Gaining knowledge: I like sex a lot—especially since I found out women are supposed to have orgasms.

Tolerance: Skinny people piss me off. Especially when they say things like, 'You know, sometimes I forget to eat.' Now, I've forgotten my address, my mother's maiden name, my money, and my keys. But I've never forgotten to eat. You have to be a special kind of stupid to forget to eat. And fuck you! In that case, you don't deserve to eat.

Weird thoughts: Why do dead people get to ride in such nice cars? That can really piss you off when you're on the bus.

> *'Why do dead people get to ride in such nice cars? That can really piss you off when you're on the bus.'*

It's not easy to get a straight answer out of Gilbert Gottfried. In fact, it's virtually impossible. As proof, take this attempt to determine his age.

"Well, I'll tell you," he starts off, "you're only as old as you feel."

And how old is that?

"I'm on my fifty-ninth facelift," Gilbert continues. "Pretty soon I'm going to get one of those facelifts where my eyes look surprised every day."

C'mon, seriously now.

"I'm older than Molly Ringwald but younger than Joan Collins."

It doesn't end there—and it doesn't end with a definite number either. But what else can you expect from a guy who says he developed his trademark squint when "someone grabbed my testicles"?

Hell, even serious career turns are given a rather flippant twist. There was, for instance, that episode more than a decade ago, when Gottfried, a poster child for manic behavior if there ever was one, was let go by the producers at "Saturday Night Live" after a mere thirteen weeks.

"I came in one day," he recalls, "and this goes back to 1980 when Joe Piscopo couldn't even lift five thousand pounds, and I went over to this desk where they used to put our fan mail, and I picked up one letter from this girl in Seattle or Wyoming or some other, like, non-Jewish state. So this girl wrote, 'Dear Gilbert, I'm so sorry about what happened to you.'

"And that," he concludes with a laugh, "is how I found out that I had been fired."

And just how did that girl find out first?

"Obviously, the producers made the decision before they told me. And then they sent letters to all the churches."

We rest our case. In his defense, however, he just can't help himself. Other small-screen disappointments, you see, are given the same treatment. In particular, there were those three TV pilots that he starred in.

The best of the lot, Gottfried figures, was "Norman's Corner"—which enjoyed a single airing on Cinemax a few years ago. The worst was a nameless network try-out that he dismisses with a shrug. Finally, somewhere in the middle, was an outing called "Toast of Manhattan," which featured three orangutans.

"One of the orangutans," he says, laughing, "actually got his own show later on called 'Mr. Smith.' Then they wound up reading me for a part in it, and then they didn't want me. Like the orangutan had bad memories or something and didn't want to work with me again."

Still, even though he figures that "Buddy Holly had better pilots than I did," Gottfried insists that he isn't turned off by television. "When somebody waves a dollar in my face, I sort of run in that direction."

And despite his contention that his first stand-up set "was rock bottom and it's never gone up," Gottfried can at least take solace in the fact that club audiences, most times, are absolutely delighted by his psychotic meanderings. He could, but he won't. After all, he wouldn't be Gilbert if he took comfort in anything so intangible. "I'm discouraged every moment of my life," he says, trying to stifle a grin. "Sylvia Plath even told me to lighten up."

GILBERT ON. . . .

The Lindbergh baby: He wasn't killed, he just got lost in luggage.

Surviving a disaster: I crashed over the Andes Mountains but I never ate a soccer player. But I brought one along just in case.

I remember the plane crash, we're sitting around in the snow and someone said, 'Look, we're here, we're hungry, let's break open the soccer player.'

I said, 'C'mon, you didn't even touch the pilot!'

gilbert gottfried

Tough questions: Last week I was having lunch with Charles Manson and in the middle of lunch he turned to me and said, 'Is it hot in here or am I crazy?'

The Old Testament: Most people don't know this but if you flip the corners of the pages like a flip book, you can see Jesus riding a horse. On the other side, there's a fat lady with a hula hoop. Most people back then thought the fat lady with the hula hoop was gonna be the famous one. I mean, nobody thought Jesus was going anywhere . . . . Where's he going? The fat lady with the hula hoop is good. . . . It's entertaining. Him, with the beard, he's maudlin, that's what he is! But, as things turned out, Jesus became more famous. Had the fat lady with the hula hoop become the famous one you'd wake up in the middle of the night, stub your toe, and scream, 'Fat lady with a hula hoop! Owwww! FAT LADY WITH A HULA HOOP!'

> *'I crashed over the Andes Mountains but I never ate a soccer player. But I brought one along just in case.'*

Carol Leifer did not pick the kind of career that a nice girl from Long Island is supposed to choose—especially not *this* particular nice girl from Long Island. After all, Dad is an ophthalmologist, Mom is a psychoanalyst, Brother is a psychiatrist, and her Ph.D. carrying sister is a linguist. All of which, so the family of doctors thought, were good jobs. On the other hand, going on stage at three in the morning and telling jokes—to people who were probably too tired or too drunk to heckle—was not what they considered to be a good job. Of this they were quite sure.

Carol, however, was also certain. She liked this choice the best. So, one night in 1978, she climbed onto the stage at New York's Comic Strip and went for it. And she was surrounded by some pretty good company.

"Jerry Seinfeld," she remembers, "was the emcee on my audition night. And I passed on the same night that Paul Reiser and Rich Hall did."

carol leifer

It was a pretty heady time for the woman who had just graduated from a college whose toughest requirement was "you had to have a number-two pencil." Soon afterwards, however, Carol found that comedy wasn't all she hoped it would be, and at that point she began to re-examine her career options.

"A couple of years into it," she explains with a rather wistful smile, "I thought about getting out of comedy and I actually sent for law school applications. I mean, at the beginning, you always have those feelings because, at first, you have to suck. It's inevitable."

Leifer persevered, however, and her career started turning around. Headlining gigs on the road were followed by guest shots on Carson and Letterman and these, in turn, led to three of her own cable specials (one on Cinemax and two on Showtime). People were definitely starting to take notice of her—even the other members of her family.

"My mother confided in me a couple of years ago," she recalls, "that they're happy now with the way things worked out. But she did tell me that she thought I would have gotten it out of my system at the beginning."

Carol didn't, of course, and as her career grew so did her circle of friends in the business. In fact, in the 1980s, Leifer, who is Jewish, married (and is now divorced from) comic Ritch Shydner, a Southern Baptist. ("My mother," she jokes, "handled it well—'He's a Nazi!'") But of all her friends she credits Jay Leno with giving her the very best piece of comedy counsel that she ever received.

"Whenever I think of advice," she says, "I can quote Jay on a million things. But I think the best thing he ever said to me was 'Don't ever remind an audience that you only work twenty minutes a day. They probably worked eight hours, came out to a show, they're tired and the last thing they want to hear is how easy *your* job is.'"

Well, it's not always *that* easy. Among other things, Carol, who can remember the dates of—and the outfits she wore for—every one of her twenty-or-so "Tonight Show" and "Late Night" appearances, does have her wardrobe problems. While the selection is rather chic and decidedly varied, she usually shies away from skirts because of the footwear they require.

"I don't like to wear heels on stage," she says, adding with a chuckle, "because if they don't like me, I like to know that I can run."

CAROL ON. . . .

Staying in shape: I'm just not into working out. Basically, my theory is no pain, ha!, no pain. But I once tried that Jane Fonda tape—*Barbarella*.

Finding the right guy: Most women like the strong, silent type. Not me. I like 'em weak and

chatty. He's 99 pounds, I can't get a word in edgewise—I'm happy.

Starting a family: I'd like to have kids one day. I want to be called 'Mommie' by someone other than Spanish guys on the streets.

Divorce—comedian style: I was part of a mixed marriage. I'm human, he's a Klingon.

Road gigs: The Pope is going to be making another world tour. He's opening for Metallica.

Television commercials: 'Impulse Body Spray—don't be surprised if a man you don't even know buys you flowers.' Great! A perfume that attracts Moonies!

Nepotism at its worst: I went to see Paul McCartney in concert. It was great. Now, the good thing is you get to see Paul. The bad thing is you have to see Linda McCartney. And just why is she in the band? You'll never see Frank Sinatra do that. You'll never see, 'And, now, on trumpet, my lovely wife, Barbara.'

'The first question a gynecologist always asks is "What was the first day of your last period?" I'm like, "I don't know, ask my dry cleaner."'

Personal questions: The first question a gynecologist always asks is 'What was the first day of your last period?' I'm like, 'I don't know, ask my dry cleaner.'

For his first cable special, a Showtime outing in early 1991, Paul Provenza decided to explore what is best known as a young man's awkward age. It's that period in a guy's life when he is, on the one hand, not able to let go of the past, but, on the other hand, not prepared to totally grab hold of the future—that confusing, exhilarating, frustrating time when feelings of insecurity hit head-on with urges to explore. It's the kind of thing that teenagers have to deal with every day. That Provenza was thirty-something at the time, however, only made it that much more awkward.

"I'm half-man, half-boy," he said shortly before the show's January airdate. "I'm just not quite sure which. I feel like a freak, but I kind of like being in this in-between place. I think it's pretty interesting."

And, it should be noted, for him that in between place could almost be summed up as to breed or not to breed. Girlfriends, he thought, were panting him into a corner and he just wasn't sure if he was ready for that kind of commitment (even though Provenza believes that he could be a great father as soon as "Purina comes out with a dry, crunchy baby food. When you can leave a bowl on the floor and go away for a week—you're looking at father of the year."). Hell, he was still lamenting all of his own unfulfilled childhood longings ("What do you say," he urged the crowd at one point, "let's run with scissors! The good ones! And we won't put them back where we found them!").

"I realized I could avoid the biological clock thing entirely," he said on stage, "by dating younger women. But you have to be careful with younger women—you don't want to be, like, a felon. So I have a rule: She has to be old enough to remember where she was when Kennedy was shot. But I find myself bending the rule. If she's really cute, 'Okay, Bobby.'"

paul provenza

And the largely thirty-ish audience at the Showtime taping absolutely ate it up. They sensed that this man/boy (who not-so-coincidentally shares Peter Pan's initials) was speaking from the heart. Afterwards, he assured them that he was.

"All the stuff that I do," he said, "is from my life. It's got to be true to me. I don't do anything just because it's funny."

Once upon a time, however. . . .

Long before Paul had ever climbed onto a nightclub stage, he was doing funny things. He figured he had to. In fact, it was almost as if he had been born to it.

"I was a pretty awkward kid," he reports. "I had a lazy eye and I wore an eye patch for a long time. Also, I was a tall, gangly kid so I was always knocking into things and knocking them over and stepping on people's toes. I was like this gawky . . . I *was* Jerry Lewis!"

Jerry, after all, did all those same things and got laughs for his trouble; so Paul decided that was the way to go. What's more, he already had the look that Lewis sported during the early years of his career.

"My grandfather," Provenza continues, "was a barber and my father was in the military. So, in the sixties, when everybody else was growing their hair long, I had these buzz-cuts from hell—these haircuts by an old man with a shaky hand being instructed by a very conservative military guy.

"What else could I do? I had to be funny. It was the only way I could distinguish myself."

PAUL ON . . . .

Evening sickness: Childhood friends of mine come up to me and tell me they're having a baby. I'm like, 'What are you talking about? You were vomiting in the bushes a week ago.'

How time flies: I know the Chinese Year of the Horse is almost over but I keep writing Snake on all my checks.

Turning thirty: Your reaction time slows down. It's that momentary lag time between when your brain realizes you've got easy listening on the radio to when your hand actually goes, 'What the hell is this shit?'

Bran new diets: Breakfast used to be fun. I used to pick my cereal for the prize inside. Now, I pick it for the prize at the bottom of my toilet bowl.

Coming of age: I find myself interested in commercials I never would have looked at before. 'You mean it comes in ointment *and* suppository?'

Landmark accomplishments: Albert Einstein figured out the theory of relativity at twenty-five. Isaac Newton at twenty-five years old discovered gravity. You know what I discovered last week? Heathcliff and Garfield are two different cats.

'I know the Chinese Year of the Horse is almost over but I keep writing Snake on all my checks.'

Being gun shy: The NRA objects to a waiting period to get a gun. Anyone who needs a gun *now,* needs a waiting period!

Smoking: If you saw that warning label on any other product you wouldn't go near it. It's like looking at the warning label on Drano—'Harmful or fatal if swallowed'—and thinking, 'Well, I'm down to three cans a week. It relaxes me.'

Rich Hall's big break came in 1980, when he stormed into New York's Improvisation Comedy Club dressed in an apron, carrying a large pizza box and sporting a huge attitude. Who, he demanded of the crowd, ordered the pie? And, more important, who didn't want to pay for it? This character, whom he describes as "sort of a Vietnam vet who was kind of on the edge," wanted answers and he wanted them immediately. *Like NOW, deadbeats!*

The bit went over real well. One guy in the audience liked it so much, in fact, that he hired Hall as a writer for his new morning show. That guy happened to be David Letterman and Rich worked for him for about a year. "The show, he says, "was really fun to do—especially after we knew that it was going to be cancelled. And then we went crazy."

You just gotta trust him on that—'cause if anyone knows from crazy, it's this guy.

Hall was born and raised in Charlotte, North Carolina, which was a place, he says, where "most people were either evangelists or truck drivers." Not fitting into either category, he headed north for college and landed in Seattle, where he studied journalism. After graduation, however, he set out on an altogether different career track—he became a street performer.

"One of the first street performers I ever saw was ['Night Court' star] Harry Anderson, who was doing insult magic. It was the coolest thing I ever saw—especially," he points out with a little chuckle, "when I saw him pass around a bucket and make all of that money!"

To get in on the action, Rich bought an old movie camera, and took it out to the streets. After a crowd had gathered, he would tell them that he had to finish a horror movie and needed their help to do so. "I would hand out scripts," he recalls, "and direct the people. I had all these people running around screaming. It got really nuts sometimes."

After "just drifting around the country" for a spell, the then-twenty-four-year-old Hall made his way to the Big Apple on July 4, 1979, and immediately set up shop in front of Lincoln Center. He got only half-way through his first show on the sidewalks of New York, however, before the cops sent him packing. It was then that he decided to get his act together and take it *off* the road. A couple of nights later he made his indoor stage debut at the Comic Strip. It was, he figures, an inevitable move.

"There aren't a lot of places to go with street performance," says Hall, who now splits his at-home time between an apartment in Los Angeles and a 114-acre ranch in Montana, "unless you work your way up to the interstate level."

But even that, at times, seemed an easier road to take than the one he chose. You see, when Rich first started doing stand-up, there weren't a lot of comedy clubs around. So Hall, like most of his peers, found himself opening for a lot of musical acts. These were not always easy gigs.

r i c h   h a l l

"You had to win over these rock fans," he says with a slight shudder. So Rich looked for ways to manipulate the audiences. "I'd try to do that with a lot of bright, shiny objects. And I used to stand behind the bass drum—figuring if they really liked the band, they wouldn't throw stuff at me and risk hurting the equipment."

There was one night in particular, though, that things really hit rock bottom. It was St. Patrick's Day, 1980, Hall was on Long Island and was opening for The Band's Levon Helm. He was performing a bit about a biker and his girlfriend that he used to do with a doll. At one point in that piece of material, he would say his girlfriend had left him and, to symbolize the event, he'd fling the doll into the audience.

"Invariably," he says, "someone in the au-

dience always threw it back. They always caught on."

This crowd was a bit slower so it took a little prodding. But finally, Hall got his doll back—though a little worse for wear.

"The thing came up in pieces. A leg comes up, a severed head, an arm stuck in a beer can. Someone started screaming, 'Fuck the doll! Fuck the doll!' and then someone else started pouring green beer on my shoe. It was," he concludes, "a nightmare."

Hall's been through a lot of career moves since then—he's an alumnus of "Saturday Night Live" and "Not Necessarily the News," and he's the author of all those *Sniglet* books. Still, despite shows like that one on St. Patrick's Day, and regardless of what other turns his career might take, he vows that he'll never give up on stand-up. "I like doing it," he says. "It's instant gratification."

Well, most of the time, anyway.

‘There aren't a lot of places to go with street performance unless you work your way up to the interstate level.’

Chris Rock's heroes at the time were Sugar Ray Leonard and Eddie Murphy. But, as he points out, since he "didn't know how to fight," comedy became the thing. And he proved so successful at the thing that in 1990, at the tender age of twenty-three, Chris became a regular on "Saturday Night Live."

"I always looked at stand-up," says the Brooklyn native, "like it was college. I figured four years, and I'll be on television. I didn't know any better."

In fact, it looks like he *did* know. Chris got the Not-Ready-for-Prime-Time gig, you see, almost exactly four years after he stepped on stage for the first time at Catch a Rising Star. "I'm a lucky guy, aren't I?" he asks rhetorically. "I'm so glad I got 'Saturday Night Live' because it's the only TV job I ever wanted. I never wanted to be the wacky neighbor."

There's little chance any Hollywood producer would ever think of Rock for that kind of a role. The guy definitely

chris rock

has a hard edge to his comedy—an edge that he often points toward racial inequities. Take, for instance, his on-stage assessment of forced school busing: "I had to get up at six o'clock in the morning to compete with white kids who got up at eight."

"When I do my racist stuff," he says, "it's different from a lot of other black comics' material because I'm actually a guy who was around white people."

And many of those white people, Rock points out, weren't always thrilled that he was there. Throughout his school days he was bused from his predominantly black neighborhood, Bedford-Stuyvesant, to attend classes in poor white areas where he would suffer through racial slurs, occasional violence, and finally, in high school, a full-fledged race riot. "Me and Andrew Dice Clay," Chris says, "went to all the same schools

—but he went about ten years ahead of me. I'm serious. You think I got like this by mistake?"

It was the riot, incidentally, that prompted Rock to drop out of school in his junior year—though he did get his GED six months later because he "didn't want to get thrown out of the house." Still, with all that has happened, Chris, who's the oldest of seven children, insists that things weren't all bad. "I had a nice childhood," he says now. "I had two parents who lived with me—which is very rare in a black neighborhood. I think I was the only one on my block whose father was still living with them.

"But I always wished my parents were divorced," he continues with a laugh, "because unlike the kids whose fathers only came around to give them presents, I never had a hundred-dollar bill."

Those would come later. While working as a busboy at a Red Lobster ("Why busboy?" he asks, "because I took the bus home, that's why") Rock got the urge to perform. His inspiration was an unsuccessful attempt to buy tickets to one of Eddie Murphy's shows at Radio City Music Hall. "It was the biggest line I ever saw," remembers Rock. "And besides being on stage, two things get me really excited—long lines and tremendous ovations."

In order to fuel his desire, Chris began sneaking out of the house at night and heading into Manhattan to try his luck at stand-up. His parents (his late father was a truck driver for the *New York Daily News* and his mother worked with retarded children) were not too happy those first few months.

"They thought I was on drugs," he says with a chuckle. "But when they found out I was only doing comedy at night I didn't get any flak from them—because everybody else *was* on drugs."

CHRIS ON. . . .

Hair fads: What is this weave bullshit? Who

said, 'You know what I like in a woman? A whole mess of fake hair.'

Washington Mayor Marion Barry: A damn mayor is on the pipe. What kind of shit is that? That's the most embarrassing shit going. . . . And trying to get some pussy at the same time! . . . That shit is *ig'nant!* And his wife is still with him! Why? He can't have no money—he's on the pipe. She must be smoking crack too.

Racial differences: I don't know everything but I think being white is like always having five dollars. And being black is like being fifty cents short.

'I don't know everything but I think being white is like always having five dollars. And being black is like being fifty cents short.'

Childhood perks: Allowance? I was *allowed* to go out of the house.

Salary philosophy: You know what it means when they pay you minimum wage? 'Hey, fuck it! If I could pay you less I would—but it's against the law.'

I t was 1967, our involvement in Vietnam was escalating, and Dennis Wolfberg had just graduated—so he no longer had a college deferment. He assessed the situation and decided that he would pack off to the jungle—the blackboard kind.

"It was an alternative," Dennis says. "There was both a war on and a teachers shortage and so it made some sense. They needed teachers and I needed safety. So I thought, there's a marriage. And it was a marriage that lasted twelve years."

Like many marriages, however, this one got off to a rather rocky start. He was assigned to an inner-city school in a section of town he describes as a "kind of war-torn area" and was greeted on opening day by picketers in front of the building.

"The first day I taught," he recalls, "was the year we had a teachers' strike over salary. "It was a three-week strike, but I couldn't strike because my name had been sent to the draft board. So I had to go in.

dennis wolfberg

"So," he continues with bulging eyes, flying hands, and a tounge that races across his lips at breathtaking speed, "the school was chaotic and they put me in with a group of fourth, fifth, and sixth grade kids, mishmashed together. In twenty minutes I lost my voice screaming at them. After that I decided, 'I'm not going in tomorrow, I don't care. Let them draft me—I'll go to Hanoi before I do this again.'"

He didn't go in that next day, but he also didn't go to Hanoi. Instead, he played golf—after calling the school to say that his grandfather (who had been dead for about ten years by then) had had a stroke.

On Wednesday, Grandpa "passed away" again. Finally, on Thursday, Dennis reported for duty once more. "I had to go in," he confesses. "They gave me a much better group of kids that day. Good kids. The kind that might end up in low-security prison."

In 1974 he earned a master's degree in psychology, but unable to get into a Ph.D. program, he re-examined his life. He knew that teaching was not something he wanted to do forever; show biz, however, held a certain fascination. So he spent his summer hiatus putting together an act of sixty jokes, and, after the first day of school that fall, he climbed onto a stage for the first time at New York's Catch a Rising Star. It did not go well.

"I had thirty friends in the audience," he remembers. "Talk about humiliation! I got off the stage, walked out, walked around the block, and retired from show business. Literally."

Well, call it semi-retirement. Four months passed before he tried his luck again, this time at the Comic Strip. And he went armed with a guitar.

"I would do a song and then tell a joke," he says with a grin. "And if they laughed at the joke, I'd tell another. If they didn't, I'd play another song. Of course I was doing a lot more singing in those days."

In 1979, Wolfberg finally stopped teaching and took comedy on full-time. And, he says, he has never looked back. In fact, he isn't even surprised by his delayed timing.

"I've always done everything late," he explains. "I got into this business when I was, like, thirty, I got married when I was thirty-nine [to comic Jeannie McBride], and I had a child when I was forty-one. I've always been a late bloomer.

"I was bar mitzvahed when I was nineteen," he jokes, "so I think that set the pattern right there."

DENNIS ON. . . .

Dating: I was not very successful. Some men have 'it'—whatever it is, it's indefinable. It's like a chemical reaction that will excite women by their mere presence. I had the antidote to whatever this thing was. I would induce restraint.

Life before marriage: The Bible says premarital sex is a sin. My wife says the way I did it, it was a crime!

Nursing: It's not easy and the child is not nibbling—he latches on pretty goddamned good, believe me. He latches on so he can't be dislodged with a crowbar once he works up a head of steam. Number one: He derives sustenance. Number two: Instinctively, he knows it's not going to get any better than this.

Respect: On the first day of school one year, one kid called me 'Wolfshit.' I said, 'The name's not Wolfshit, it's Wolfberg, and what's more, it's Mr. Wolfberg.' And the kid said, 'How am I supposed to know you're married?'

The name game: Were we to have a girl, my wife wanted to call her Sue, which is a lovely name, but which for Jews is generally a verb.

> **'Were we to have a girl, my wife wanted to call her Sue, which is a lovely name, but which for Jews is generally a verb.'**

Medical advances: We found out my wife had an ovarian cyst. Which didn't bother me nearly as much as the fact that she found this out from her dentist.

Student absenteeism: They would come in with the most brazen excuses. One kid, who returned after being out for two days, told me he had had a stroke. Back after two days! What a remarkable commitment to education!

Teaching in the South Bronx: This was the only school I know of with its own coroner. The school newspaper had an obituary column. I used to assign compositions like 'What I want to be if I grow up!'

When Carrie Snow remembers events in her life it's like listening to someone recount favorite sitcom episodes; everything has a set-up and a punchline. And, insists the woman whose motto is "Seven thousand sailors can't be wrong," it's all true.

Take, for instance, these scenes from her childhood. Born in San Francisco and raised in Merced, California, Carrie Pelletz Snow was a gifted child who attended special classes and was therefore always under the watchful eyes of the doctors and educators who studied children with minds like hers. Just how advanced was she at that time? "A psychologist," Snow says with a hearty laugh, "once told my parents never to sign anything over to me because I'd own them."

It should be pointed out that her parents (a travelling salesman father and a "housewife-painter-irritant" mother) never did sign anything over to her. They did, however, send her to college at Berkeley, where she graduated with a degree in rhetoric. Considering her major, it's no surprise she can sum up those four years so succinctly: "I went to classes, worked, fucked around, learned about life, had a great time, and slept with guys that I couldn't pick out of a line-up now."

From there Snow, who once answered a personal ad that read, "submissive male wants to clean house for attractive, dominant female—no charge, no strings" ("he was good but I had to be there," she bitches), went to graduate school "for about five minutes" before getting day jobs as a librarian and a receptionist for a medical research lab (where her nametag read "C. Snow P."). But she had a hankering for something more creative, so she and a friend started a professional party guest service—her job was to spice up private soirées. To accomplish that, the then-amply proportioned Snow would dress up as Shirley Temple and warble song parodies like "You Louse Up My Life."

That episode was followed by another stab at entrepreneurism. Snow, who's a clotheshorse and an incredibly dedicated shopper ("They have it, I want it"), entered the design field—with yet another friend. This time the product was crotchless panties, and with three sewing machines whirring (the friend's sister also got involved), they readied their first panty line for Valentine's Day and hawked their goods on San Francisco's wharf. By February 15th, however, after a mere two days in retail, they folded up shop. Still, Snow (who used to emcee male strip shows) is sure that she is not a forgotten designer. Because of the wharf's high tourism rate, "I just know that me and my panties are in slide shows all across this country," she says with a satisfied smile.

Even if they're not, Carrie, at least, has finally made it to the four corners of the country with her stand-up. And since leaving her day job in '79, she says that she has never looked back.

Not even that time in Florida a few years ago made her regret her choice. She was performing at a charity benefit in the ballroom of a hotel (the hardest type of setting to work, according to comics), and one of the guests walked up to her and said that he'd donate $5,000 to the charity if she would shut her mouth and not say another word. With that, Snow dropped the mike, walked out of the room, and burst into tears.

"It was *so* horrible," she reports, "that I had to give away the outfit I was wearing. My boyfriend at the time told me I should have asked him how much he would have paid me to get out of the business entirely."

It would have to be a high price, indeed. Carrie, you see, loves what she does. "No matter how bad things get," she once said, "it still beats the hell out of weighing nuts at Woolworth's."

carrie snow

CARRIE ON. . . .

Career moves: If I could blow my way to the top, I'd already be there.

The name game: When I saw *Dances With Wolves* I couldn't decide which Indian name I wanted for myself. It was a toss-up between 'Dry Scalp' and 'Touches Herself.'

Marriage: I once told my father that I didn't think I could be polite enough for long enough to get married. He told me, 'You only have to be nice for a couple of months. And then you can turn on them like a cur dog—just like your mother did to me.'

Milestones: I'm reaching my sexual peak and it's lonely at the top. . . . The last time I got laid, AIDS was still that shitty diet candy.

Relation slips: My cousin Nancy bought Christmas cards from the Alzheimer's Foundation, and then she forgot to send them out.

Reproduction: I have a friend who is so hairy, if he fathered a girl child, you'd have to kill it.

Tricks and treats: You know why God is a man? Because if God was a woman she would have made sperm taste like chocolate. It gives a whole new meaning to Nestle's Quick.

> *When I saw Dances with Wolves I couldn't decide which Indian name I wanted for myself. It was a toss-up between "Dry Scalp" and "Touches Herself."*

Born Pablo Leobordo Castro Gutierrez Rodriguez in Mazatlan, Mexico, the son of poor migrant farm workers, Paul did most of his growing up in tough East Los Angeles, where his family moved when he was very young. And it was there that he honed the skills that made him a migrant worker too. Albeit, he is a very well-paid one, who travels from town to town not to pick lettuce, but to pick other, more valuable, green stuff.

"Comedy," the former gang member once told *People* magazine, "was my secret weapon. It saved my life many times. I wasn't the meanest dude in the barrio but I was the funniest."

He was also one of the luckiest—he escaped a dead-end life by joining the Air Force. It was a decision, he says, that came rather unexpectedly.

"My gang," he remembers of those days, "was in this war with another gang. And one day the guy to the left of me was shot and the guy on the right was killed. And by the grace of God I didn't get shot—so I *ran* to my recruiter."

paul rodriguez

Four years later Rodriguez, who once entertained the idea of becoming a lawyer, started taking some classes at Cal State. Eventually, though, he climbed onto a stand-up stage. It was 1981, at an amateur night at the Comedy Store in Los Angeles, when Paul decided to give joke-telling a shot. He went over well that night, immediately dropped out of school, and started making the comedy rounds—armed, it should be pointed out, with more than his ready wit.

"Do you know me?" he'd ask the audience in his early career days. "My name is Paul Rodriguez. But when I travel, people don't know who the hell I am. That's why I carry the Mexican Express card." At this point he would reveal a huge knife and conclude, "It's recognized all over the world."

These days, it's Rodriguez, whose first comedy album was called *You're in America, Speak Spanish,* who's recognized all over the world. Paul has starred in a couple of short-lived TV shows—"a.k.a. Pablo" and "Trial and Error," and his celebrity has even followed him to San Quentin prison, where he taped a Fox TV special a couple of years back. "It was weird," he says. "There were two guys who were serving life terms who I went to high school with."

Rodriguez, too, almost had a chance to serve something of a prison term—of the highly personal variety. Before taping began, you see, Rodriguez and fellow comic Elayne Boosler were sitting in a secured area when guards walked through with two shackled prisoners, and Rodriguez was struck by a fanciful urge.

"These guys," Boosler remembers, "are coming by us and all of a sudden Paul grabs me and says to one of the prisoners, 'Hey, man, how many cigarettes will you give me for her?' I couldn't believe it. And then the guy tells Paul, 'No offense, but I don't like women anymore but I'll give you a carton if *you* spend the night with me!' It was hysterical—I thought Paul was gonna die."

He didn't. Instead, Rodriguez went on stage that night and killed. He also broke the rules.

"The officials told us," he recalls, "that we couldn't go into the audience because they couldn't guarantee our protection. But everyone was having so much fun that I forgot about the rules and jumped into the audience. Hey," he says with a laugh, "I felt safer among them than I do when I get stopped in my car by the Los Angeles police department."

PAUL ON. . . .

Flying the unfriendly skies: It's a pleasure to be here—but hell, when you fly Delta Airlines, it's a pleasure to be anywhere. . . .

Where do these stewardesses get this holier-than-thou attitude? 'Bring your seats up to a very uncomfortable position, goddamnit!' Let's face

it, if they were on the ground, they'd be waitresses at McDonald's. . . .

They tell you things like, 'Make sure you know where your exits are.' I figure, if this thing hits the ground, there will be plenty of gaping holes for me to get out of. . . .

They actually tell you this: 'Ladies and gentlemen, in case of emergency, place your head between your legs.' Who are they kidding? If I could do that, I'd never leave the house.

Modern sex: I'm from Los Angeles. There are so many diseases there, I don't even touch myself anymore. I'm so paranoid that when I go to the bathroom to take a piss, I use a pair of tongs from the kitchen to hold my dick—*because I know where I've been.*

The worst kind of nights: I had a nightmare the other night. I woke up, Jim Nabors was buckling my belt.

> *'The other day I went to a Mexican restaurant run by a black family. It's called Casa Yo Mama. They don't have menus or nothing. A dude named Calvin comes and tells you what you gonna have.'*

Eating out: The other day I went to a Mexican restaurant run by a black family. It's called Casa Yo Mama. They don't have menus or nothing. A dude named Calvin comes and tells you what you gonna have.

A Whitney Brown's life reads like a psychedelic soap opera—with equal parts borrowed from *Easy Rider*, Jack Kerouac's *On the Road*, and *I Was a Fugitive from a Chain Gang*. Still, and despite the occasional shake of the head, the man who's known as the "Big Picture" commentator on "Saturday Night Live," recites it all as if it were the sort of thing that happens to everybody.

It started when he left his broken home at the age of fourteen. This was not entirely his idea; his father had something to do with it as well. "He sold me up the river is what he did," Brown insists with the straightest face possible. "He'd lock me in a cabin and then he'd go off and get drunk in a tankard and live in a hogshead, goddamnit. And he took me away from the Widow Douglas. Oh . . ." he pauses, cracking a little smile, "That wasn't me."

No, that was Huckleberry Finn—but Brown's own story could make for a book as well. "Actually," he continues, apparently seriously now, "what he did was he turned me over to the state as an incorrigible. He made me a ward of the state, which put me in prison, basically.

"Anyway," he concludes with a shrug, "I spent a little time there and escaped. I ran away. Well, I didn't really run away—no one really missed me."

The first leg of his on-the-lam journey brought him to Canada, where he posed as an American draft dodger in order to get free food and clothes. "It was probably the lowest thing I've ever done in my life."

Not that everything that followed was so admirable. After a year or so up north, Brown headed back into the States where he "hitched all over the place" and supported himself by selling drugs at rock concerts. One such event was Woodstock.

a. whitney brown

"You may have seen me in the movie," he jokes. "I was the guy with the tarp on his head." While the show lasted a mere weekend, Brown hung out at the upstate New York concert site for about three weeks and, he insists, "can still remember most of it," even though he "took every drug" he could get his hands on.

"I was definitely an acid head," says Brown, who is now chemically independent. "But I think acid really did save me, actually. I think I would have been a petty criminal if it hadn't been for LSD. It showed me such a big world out there. Or such a big world in there. Or something.

"I never had any idea," he says with a slight smile. "It humbled me. It really did—it made me realize that I should get my shit together because I was a punk, and boy, when you take LSD, that humbles you. 'Please, Lord, I promise I'll be good.'"

Not that he was, mind you. Among other careless episodes, there was that little ol' scrape with the law in Texas. All he was doing, he insists, was driving through the Lone Star State en route to California, when he got stopped by police merely because he had "long hair and northern licence plates." He also had a couple of joints of pot in his possession and those, he says, earned him an eighteen-month jail term.

"That was my last road trip. That was the last time I was ever in jail. Those Texas people will teach you respect for the law. It was," he says with a laugh, "an experience. And it does teach you a sense of humor."

Which finally brings us to San Francisco, where in the mid '70s, Brown started out as a street juggler, graduating to comedy a few years later. "It was 1978," he remembers, "when I did stand-up for the first time. I did five minutes of pure stand-up without juggling. Before that," he concludes, "I just couldn't drop the balls."

A. WHITNEY ON. . . .

Urban living: It's not easy being black in New York City for numerous reasons. Taxis won't stop for you, every crackhead panhandler thinks he can call you 'brother' and, on top of all that, you have to open the paper every other morning and read that Al Sharpton has just appointed himself your spokesman.

The war in the Gulf: If Vietnam was the first television war, this is the first Nintendo war. Whoever thought Pong would lead to this? . . . . France is behind us on this—and that's probably where they'll be, too. Actually, I think they'll fight this time. They have to. They want to prove that winning that war against Greenpeace was no fluke. . . . George Bush said he was going to be 'the education president.' We just didn't know it was Saddam Hussein he was going to teach a lesson to. . . . These new bombs are smarter than most of our high school graduates. At least they can find Kuwait on a map. If they make them any smarter, they'll start having second thoughts about war itself.

> *'These new bombs are smarter than most of our high school graduates. At least they can find Kuwait on a map.'*

Louie Anderson did not have an enviable childhood. In fact, as presented by the Minneapolis-born comic, his dysfunctional family's portrait was more the work of Salvador Dali than Norman Rockwell, with the harshest brush strokes supplied by his father's alcoholism.

As described in Anderson's 1989 book, *Dear Dad: Letters from an Adult Child*, young Louie's daily home life held but one constant—Dad's random ugliness. The old man's inability to hold a job, his erratic fits of violence, and his frightening mood-swings provided the fare that made up the family's emotional diet.

And while Louie, Sr., took solace from a bottle, Louie, Jr., took comfort in second and third helpings at the dinner table. But even his wall of fat couldn't protect him. Many was the night that the youngster would be lulled to sleep by the sound of Dad viciously yelling at Mom, only to be woken hours later by a drunk at the foot of his bed who was screaming, "Hey lard ass, when are you going to lose some weight?"

louie anderson

Given the situation, one could easily understand Anderson's desire to strike back at the father he alternately loved and loathed. Still, Louie insists, *Dear Dad* was not written as an act of retribution. Instead, he says, the project began shortly after his father's 1986 death from cancer as a way to tell his dad in death everything that he couldn't tell him in life.

"I wrote the letters more as a therapeutic thing for myself," Anderson explains. "Then I realized it might be just the connecting rod that somebody else might need—the thing to let them know that they're not alone."

The book also served as an avenue for Louie to let his audience know that his gentle sense of humor belied his upbringing, that he was more than a roly-poly joke machine, and that routines like the achingly funny drunk bit he performed on his first hour-long HBO special sprung from devastatingly painful roots.

In addition to coming to grips with the aftermath of his father's decidedly negative influence, Louie, who has worked with emotionally disturbed children, is also trying to get a handle on his weight problem. "Food is my substance abuse," he explains." That's my addiction.

"But," he adds, "I'm learning how to deal with that. I'm fat, but I'm on the road to recovery."

To that well-intentioned end, Anderson, who used to open shows by moving the mike stand from the front of the stage to the back ("so that you can see me better"), has stopped doing the self-deprecating fat jokes that once served as the cornerstone of his act. "I think they hurt in the long run," he explains, "because they reinforce something deep inside."

The plan, he says, is to write a book about being fat in America ("And I'm going to tell the truth about that too," he vows) and, eventually, to leave the stand-up stage behind. "I'm trying to work my way out of show business," he says. "I think that's the best thing you can do, to try to get out of something after you've become good at it and then to move onto something else. That's what the sign of life is for me—to keep growing."

LOUIE ON. . . .

Career choices: The worst job is that Fotomat job. Where do these people take their breaks? Do they duck down?

Natural disasters: One thing I don't understand—flood areas. Why would you want to live in a flood area? After the first time, don't you get it?

Life after the nuclear holocaust, 1: There will be comedy clubs, but what will be funny? Can you imagine working really hard on a joke, getting ready to deliver the punchline, all of a sudden, there's a guy in the front row, his foot falls off? How do you top that?

Life in Hollywood: I live in California, the worst place in the world for fat people. There are three of us. They have us on eight-hour shifts, so it works out.

Whale watching: I can't get into that California lifestyle. I was at the beach and every time I would lie down people would push me back in the water. 'Hurry up, he's dying.'

Timing: Listen, I can't stay long; I'm in between meals.

Stupor stupidity: I like when drunks get philosophical. 'Hey, Louie! Life! Live it!'

Life after the nuclear holocaust, 2: Men won't change. Like with dating. 'She's not *too* badly burned.' And you'll all be following me around. 'He knows where food is.'

> **'I live in California, the worst place in the world for fat people. There are three of us. They have us on eight-hour shifts, so it works out.'**

Andrew Dice Clay is the antithesis of the modern man. He stands on stage, hair slicked back, sideburns below the ears, a study in biker black that is broken only by the huge silver belt buckle and sterling studs that adorn his leather jacket. He is a hardened, chain-smoking '50s icon somehow misplaced in this later, more sensitive decade.

The talk, as one would expect, is dock-side tough. He lectures women—whom he refers to as "pigs," "sluts," and worse—on proper sexual technique. He takes hitherto harmless nursery rhymes and transforms them into raunchy chants. He asks audience members for intimate lovemaking details. Then he gets dirty.

In otha woids, Andrew Dice Clay ain't got no couth when he's performing—which is just the way his fans love it. You only have to hear them cheer fanatically as this high priest of machismo takes his slow, calculated strut to the mike to know that.

You want further proof? Ask the Diceman. "My audiences are great," the Brooklyn College dropout insists. "They respond to me as if I'm the Beatles. It's complete mania."

No, Andrew Dice Clay, the performer, is hardly shy. But Andrew Dice Clay, the guy who grew up in Brooklyn as Andrew Silverstein, insists that it's merely a pose.

"If I was really an egomaniac," he says, pointing to Kathleen Monica, his girlfriend and the mother of his son, Max, "she could never live with me. She's a regular girl. This isn't some chick I met in Hollywood, some wannabe. This is a nice girl from Jersey.

"The thing is," he insists, "I know the difference between the person and the performer. On stage, I am not the boy next door but off stage, I am. And," he concludes, "what people should understand is that it's a joke."

Some folks, however, don't agree. His rather vocal critics have, not surprisingly, called him racist, sexist, and worst of all, banal. "Fuck 'em," he responds with a sneer. "They're just stupid, that's all that I can say."

Despite the naysayers, however, Dice is sure he'll have the last laugh. "I am going to be the biggest," he says with characteristic bravado.

Still, no matter how big he becomes, Clay has taken measures to ensure that he'll never forget his roots. While he keeps a house in Los Angeles, he maintains his primary residence in Brooklyn—which is where he also set up his main office. There his father, Fred, runs Clay's production company and takes care of all the money that the Dice rolls in.

And Clay, who started out on stage doing Jerry Lewis and John Travolta impersonations, insists that "I don't want to forget what it's like to be a normal person."

That may indeed be the case, but, as a former clothing salesman, he definitely enjoys his new-found buying power. "Once," he remembers, "I walked into a sporting goods store and bought a hundred pairs of socks, simply for a goof."

Still, he says, things like that won't go to his head. "When I started out, I had one vinyl motorcycle jacket. Now I have a hundred leather jackets and I appreciate every one of 'em."

He also appreciates his stardom for what it is. "No matter how big I get, I know that I'm not that important," he allows. "I'm not the President of the United States." Then, after a short pause, he adds, "Yet."

"Hey," he declares, taking a loud sip of black coffee, "why not? Look at me! I've got that Kennedy charisma."

BEDTIME WITH THE DICEMAN:
There was an old woman who lived in a shoe,
She had so many kids her fuckin' uterus fell out.

andrew dice clay

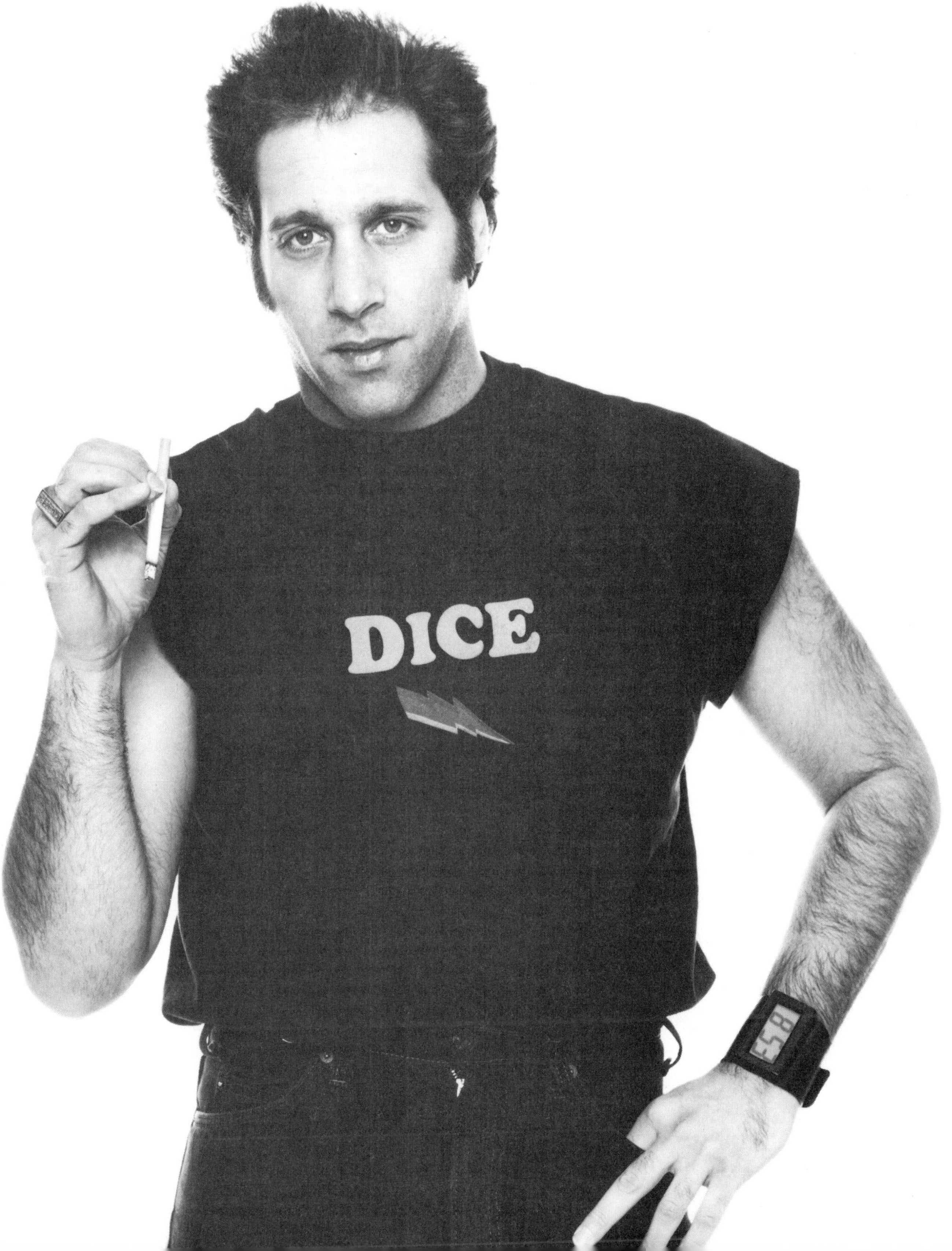
DICE

Little Miss Muffet sat on a tuffet
Eating her curds and whey.
Along came a spider, who sat down beside her,
And said, `Yo, what's in the bowl, bitch?'

Little Boy blew. . . .
Hey, he needed the money!

'Little Boy blew. . . .
Hey, he needed the money!'

Old Mother Hubbard went to the cupboard to get her old dog a bone.
When Mother bent over, Rover took over, he had a bone of his own.

Hickory dickory dock, this chick was suckin' my cock,
The clock struck two, I shot my goo,
And dropped the bitch on the next block.

Call him the comedy clairvoyant. Bobby Collins doesn't know how he knows these things, but he just does. He and fellow comic Steve Skrovan were working on a shoot for Showtime when Collins had this uncontrollable urge to wish Skrovan well on his upcoming fatherhood. Skrovan was absolutely stunned—he and his wife were indeed expecting their first child, but they had only found out about it a day earlier. They hadn't even told anyone yet.

But Bobby, who in his tailored, designer suits looks more hit-man than joke-man, wasn't done with his pronouncements. The baby, the all-knowing comic declared, would be a girl. And, sure enough, nine months later the two men ran into each other again and proud papa Skrovan announced, "Hey, Bobby, it was a boy!"

"Yeah?" responded a knowing Collins. "Well, you just better keep an eye on him."

"I know everything about everyone else," Collins says with a laugh, "but not about myself."

bobby collins

Too bad, considering a little premonition could have saved Bobby from a couple of bad nights. There was that time in Philadelphia, when a woman in the front row wearing a short skirt and no underwear spread her legs ("You try to do a show when some woman is showing you Honolulu"). And there was that other particularly gruesome night in the summer of 1990.

"Everyone has hundreds of bad gigs," he explains of that evening, "but this is the one that I wanted to send my underwear home in a manila envelope."

At that time, Collins was touring the country opening for Cher, and this show in Bristol, Connecticut, was the second of thirty that he would do with her. The first show, he reports, "was an unbelievable experience—it was great." Well, let's just say that the euphoria ended quickly.

"We're in Bristol," he recalls. "There are thirty-thousand people there. And, little did I know, that this was part of an all-day outdoor festival that started at ten A.M. was going till ten P.M. and was culminating with the eight o'clock Cher concert.

"So half the people in the audience are crocked and they don't even *know* who Cher is anymore. And when they announced me," he says with a shudder, "as soon as I walked out on stage, all of these people on the left side were booing. And I didn't even say a word yet. And then, on the right side, all of a sudden comes a chant—'We want Cher! We want Cher!'"

As it turned out, the left side of the audience was booing the security guards, who'd confiscated the beach ball that was being batted around by the crowd; the right side was genuinely anxious; and Collins, meanwhile, was shaken.

"I did my twenty-five minutes, and while doing it, three people in the front threw up. Not from my act," he clarifies, "they were drunk.

"When I got off," he concludes, "I was like, 'Honey, let's get that little McDonald's franchise we were talking about.'"

BOBBY ON. . . .

Election results: You remember when George Bush became President? They took his wife's commercial off the air. 'Clap on . . . Clap off . . . .'

Going without, part 1: My wife had a baby. She had a tough pregnancy—she was bedridden for five months. The doctor said to me, 'No sex.' I told him, 'Doc, I'm half Italian. I've got to have sex.' The doctor said, 'No sex!' I told him, 'Doc, wear something pink—I'll pick you up at eight-thirty.'

Going without, part 2: Things were so bad, I was carrying a picture of my right hand in my wallet. Finally one night, after five months, I couldn't hold out sexually anymore. My wife was dead asleep. I started to climb on her head and

unzip my pants. She wakes up and screams, 'What are you doing?' I'm like checking my pockets—'My wallet! I lost my wallet! Did you see my wallet?'

Endings: Two Jews walk into a bar. They buy it. That's it. I don't know jokes. I'm a storyteller.

'You remember when George Bush became president? They took his wife's commercial off the air. "Clap on . . . clap off. . . ." '

Larry David would show up at New York showcase clubs regularly and each time the buzz would begin. Is he going on? He's right there—ya think he'll go on? You could never be sure until he actually hit the stage considering he had a tendency, for whatever reason, to change his mind at the last minute and leave. "Yeah," says Larry, "I would do that a lot."

"When I do stand-up," he explains, "I feel very frightened, usually because I've humiliated myself so many times, and I know what that feels like. And I want to avoid it at all costs."

And he's able to do just that these days, since he's the executive producer of the NBC sitcom "Seinfeld" ("I'm not smart enough to do two things at once," he jokes). But starting as far back as 1975, he kept plugging away at stand-up—in his fashion, of course.

On those occasions when he actually did get up and stand behind the mike, his act generally went over best in the back of the room where the other comics

larry david

hung out. Back there, they always loved this guy. "I don't know why they liked me," he says, "but I'm glad they did. That's sort of what kept me going." Good thing, too, since the reaction to him in the front of the room, where the paying customers sit, was always a crap shoot.

"One night at the Improv," he remembers with a chuckle, "these four women attacked me. They wanted to fight but it was broken up when people at the bar interceded. I don't remember what I said but they obviously didn't appreciate it."

It was not an isolated incident. There were, he admits, a lot of sets that ended like that one. "I would even get attacked *during* shows," he says. "And I didn't react well to hecklers. Other comics would be able to come up with one-liners to put those people down, but I couldn't do it. I would simply yell at them. At first the audience would laugh thinking I was joking, but after five minutes they'd start to realize I was serious."

Yes, Larry David was—and is—one serious guy. But he didn't become comedy's favorite inside jokester by mistake. To begin with, he staged enough well-received sets that he "never really thought of getting out of the business."

And, too, there's his material. Take this treasure, for example: "I'd like to have a kid but I suppose I have to have a date first."

Or even, this one: "I hate women. They're so effeminate. They're like fags."

It was definitely there—he just sometimes had a tough time selling it to the audience. "If things weren't going well for me," Larry says, "I reacted like a child. I couldn't take it. I don't take criticism very well. But there's a contradiction there, because I also want to be well-liked."

David also wanted to go where no comic had gone before. "I didn't want to say things," he explains, "that anyone else could say." A perfect example was his opening routine, a bit that he always did despite the fact that it never got a lot of laughs. He would say: "In case I break into Spanish or French, may I use the familiar *tu* form with you?"

Now he says, "It never really worked very well but I kept it because I thought it was funny and it made *me* laugh. It tickled me. I thought it would be a funny way to open the act, but it really wasn't. But I continued to do it."

Didn't his peers ever give him any advice about these things?

"Oh, yeah!"

Did he ever follow it?

"No!"

"I'm able to look at my act now and understand why I didn't go over very well," he says. "I didn't understand it then. At the time, occasionally I would say things to my friends and they'd go, 'that's funny.' And I'd say, 'Well, I can't do that.' So I'd give it to them, and they'd do it and

get big laughs and I'd be bombing with my act. I couldn't quite figure it out.

"Then I realized," he concludes, "that I just have a very limited appeal."

It should be something of a comfort to him that he's always appealed to some of the best people in comedy.

'I hate women. They're so effeminate. They're like fags.'

Some people work a lifetime towards achieving a measure of fame. Some have fame thrust upon them. And some, like Calvert DeForest, just sort of step in it. And when he stepped in it, he stepped in it big time.

The sixty-something DeForest, a resident of Bay Ridge, Brooklyn, was working as a receptionist and file clerk for a drug and alcohol rehabilitation program when he got a yen for acting—just thought it would be fun. So, in order to sate his theatrical appetite, he appeared in a couple of community theater productions, and later, he even garnered a few small roles in student films. This was, however, hardly the high road to success.

But as luck would have it, one of those films, *King of the Z*, was made by two New York University students, Karl Tiedemann and Stephen Winer. And, in 1982, these young men became writers for a new show called "Late Night With David Letterman." Well, the "Late Night" producers saw the movie, enjoyed the performances, and, we like to imagine, jumped to their feet screaming: *"Get us that nebbish!"* Okay, so maybe it happened differently. No matter. Larry "Bud" Melman was born. Or, as DeForest says with a laugh, "history was made." Or, more specifically, a dupe was created.

As anyone who's ever watched DeForest go through his paces on "Late Night" knows, this is not a person we laugh with. Instead, the joke always seems to be on him. Whether he's hawking Toast-on-a-Stick, fielding ridiculous questions from the studio audience, playing a singing gardener, handing out hot towels at the Port Authority, or doing anything else, *he's* the punchline.

None of which seemed to bother him a few years back. "Doing the Letterman show," he said in 1984, "is like having a ball. It's fun time all the time."

calvert deforest, a.k.a.
larry "bud" melman

Apparently, things haven't changed, seeing as he keeps renewing his contract—despite the disastrous 1988 "Late Night"-sponsored "Calvert DeForest Pan-American Goodwill Tour," which was cut short due to a "bad stomach." For that project, DeForest left New York in a mobile home en route to Tierra Del Fuego at the southernmost tip of South America. His assignment was to meet and greet as many people as possible, spreading good cheer all along the way. By Guatemala City, however, all bets were off. In an achingly funny on-air phone call to Dave, a quite serious DeForest begged his boss to be allowed to come home. In short, a trooper he ain't.

But that is exactly his appeal. So many people can do things well. DeForest, on the other hand, just does the best he can—and usually, his best is rather inept. After all, here's a man who's a TV star because he's no good at being on TV. When the camera hits him he looks like a deer caught in the road, he can't seem to read a cue card correctly (probably not even if his life depended on it), and he never reacts well to improvised moments.

Oh, yeah, real star material! Still, other stars have noticed him. "That's something that gets me," says DeForest, "when celebrities tell you how much they enjoy you and *they're* so big themselves."

Take, for instance, this encounter he had with Bob Hope after the veteran comic made an appearance on "Late Night." "I was on," DeForest remembers, "and he watched what I did. After he went on, I stood outside the studio to get a glimpse of him. When he passed by me he shook my hand and said he was cracking up at what I had done. I thought, 'Oh, my God! Coming from Hope, the master of comedy timing, that's really praise.'"

And while he counts Pee-wee Herman and Mark Hamill as friends, he hasn't yet developed a large circle of Hollywood pals. And, in a

1988 interview, he said that he and Letterman were only "acquaintances."

"Let's say we don't go to dinner after the show. I have never been to his home in Connecticut or in Malibu. What's the point? He told me he'd lock me up if I showed up."

'I have never been to Letterman's home in Connecticut or in Malibu. What's the point? He told me he'd lock me up if I showed up.'

Margaret Smith does something totally unexpected when she's off stage. She smiles—quite a bit. And not just the anticipated little, knowing smirks. Sometimes she even breaks out in big wide grins. Granted, it's not exactly something to alert the *Guinness Book of World Records* about, but the first time this deadpan comic turns up the corners of her mouth and shows a little sliver of her perfectly white teeth, it just sets you back for a second. That's understandable, considering that she has made a name for herself as, shall we say, a decidedly less-than-chipper personality.

"Some people just don't get it," Smith has said of her on-stage persona. "They only see the anger, not the fact that I'm actually making fun of myself. And I'm really not angry. *Angry* is if I got on top of a three-story building and opened fire on a playground."

There's little chance of that—especially since she has finally found an outlet for her talent, which is something she couldn't seem to find at home. The third of six siblings, Margaret grew up in the small Chicago suburb of Mount Greenwood. From there, it was on to Chicago itself for a short stay before heading East to New York in 1981. Now the motorcycle-riding comic lives in Los Angeles.

Smith, who thinks of comedy as an art form, explains that "in big cities, art is recognized. In small places it's not. That's what cities are for—centers for art. Back home," she says, flashing one of those grins, "art came in the form of tattoos."

If you got the idea that Margaret Smith wasn't exactly thrilled with her Middle-American upbringing, you got the right impression. Continue that thought, and you'll understand that she isn't all that thrilled with her Middle-American family either. Still, she realizes that all of those things helped shape a comic vision that she refers to as "the world according to Margaret."

margaret smith

"Now," she points out, "I can talk about my horrible childhood and my horrendous family and say, 'I lived to tell about it.' Everyone has weirdos in their family. I just embrace mine."

There are certain unpalatable memories, however, that she would rather not embrace. There was, for instance, the advice she received for one of her first road trips. Margaret, who had limited her early performances to the New York area, was told by the man who was her manager at the time that she had to stop doing just her "hip stuff." She needed, he informed her, "to learn Middle America."

So Smith went forth and, she says, managed to learn three things. 1) "That everything they say about the South is true"; 2) "That when it isn't working for me on stage, not to give them more but to give them less because they don't want up here," she says, waving a delicate hand over her head, "they want here," she concludes, lowering her hand to her midsection; and finally, 3) "I learned that I hate it."

Not exactly a shock considering the source. But don't think that Margaret is like Mikey, the opinionated kid in the Life cereal commercial. There really are some things that she actually likes.

"I like people who don't really like traditional comedy," she says. "I'm the anti-comedian, I guess. It took me my whole life to get comfortable with not fitting in—and now I make money because I don't fit in."

Nice work if you can get it. And luckily, for all of those other misfits in all of those playgrounds, she did.

MARGARET ON. . . .

The 'people person' she takes after most: The inscription on my Uncle Swanee's tombstone says: 'What are *you* looking at?'

Things to look out for: Stay away from people who are into misery because misery loves company. If you don't believe me, just look at a fly

strip. You'll never see a fly stuck there saying, 'Go around! Go around.'

The hazards of picking friends: I love strangers, I really do. But there are drawbacks to that kind of attraction. I keep thinking I'm going to be sitting in a theater and some strange guy is going to walk up to me and smack me in the head and say, 'Hey! Don't you remember? You told me that if ever I saw you wearing your hair like that to smack you in the head.'

The dangers of 'hope': There's a light at the end of the tunnel. Yeah—it's a train.

Close encounters: This guy came up to me at a bar and said, 'Hey, Cupcake, can I buy you a drink?' And I said, 'No, but I'll take the three bucks.'

Her hometown: The only thing I miss about Chicago is the blues. Chicago is, like, the blues capital of the world. It's not as good in Los Angeles. I went to a blues club in L.A. the other night and there were four black guys and a white guy up on stage. They're up there with their eyes closed, jamming, getting down—and I notice the white guy peeking. . . . I got my money back.

> *This guy came up to me at a bar and said, "Hey, Cupcake, can I buy you a drink?" And I said, "No, but I'll take the three bucks."*

There are few men who can make the boast, and fewer still who would actually dare to, but Harry Shearer—and damn the venomous Hollywood tongue waggers who might condemn him for this—is one of the last. Yes, he readily admits, he was one of Jack Benny's Beavers. Not Benny's only Beaver, mind you, but "on and off for eight years" in the '50s, he was one of the few young boys that Benny called Beaver.

The whole episode started in 1950, when Shearer first met that legendary comic. He was a mere seven years old when he debuted on "The Jack Benny Radio Show," and his duties were decidedly diverse.

"Sometimes," Shearer remembers without a trace of bitterness, "I was Benny as a kid."

And it doesn't end there, folks—oh no, there's much more. "Sometimes," he continues, "I did child versions of other actors on the show.

"And sometimes" (the weak of heart had better brace themselves) "I was part of this group of kids that Benny used to squire around, sort of like a Boy Scout troop, which was called the Beverly Hills Beavers. These being more innocent times, I *was* one of his Beavers. And," Harry concludes with a rather sly laugh, "that kept me busy."

We can only imagine, ladies and gentlemen, we can only imagine. Still, insists Shearer (who played Eddie Haskell in the TV pilot for "Leave It to Beaver"—there's that word again), his memories of those formative years are fond. "Working for Benny," he says, "prepares you very badly for a career in show business. He was so smart, talented, and *sane* that it made you think that everyone in the business was like that—and they aren't."

Still, with only one extended leave of absence, he has stuck with the business. At fifteen-and-a-half he quit to study political science at UCLA, and later, he attended graduate school at Harvard for a year. Along the way, he worked as a stringer for *Newsweek* (even covering the Watts Riots for them), and in 1965 landed in the Cailfornia State Legislature as an intern. From there, he spent two years teaching school (English and social studies). "These," he instructs us, "are all called draft dodges."

By the late '60s he had hired a draft attorney, refused induction into the Army ("Nothing ever happened," he says incredulously, "and I presume the statute of limitations has lapsed"), and found himself back on radio performing satirical newscasts. In time, among other projects, he worked with a group called the Credibility Gap; co-wrote *Real Life* with Albert Brooks; was a "so-called creative consultant" on "Fernwood Tonight"; produced and starred in a network special with Martin Mull, Billy Crystal, Christopher Guest, and Tom Leopold called "The TV Show"; and directed Martin Mull's cable series, "The History of White People in America."

harry shearer

What's more, he joined the cast of "Saturday Night Live" for its 1979-80 season which he has described as "a great flying leap into hell." He followed that by co-writing and co-starring in the cult mock-rock-documentary *This Is Spinal Tap* (he was bassist Derek Smalls) and even returned to "SNL" for its 1984–85 season.

"After *Spinal Tap*, they went after Chris [Guest] and Michael [McKean] and me and only Michael had the good sense to say no. I left in the middle of that year. The producers," he explains, "had changed but the method of abusing people obviously went with the franchise."

And no, despite all we've read, he doesn't think that drugs had anything to do with the atmosphere on the "SNL" set. "I think cocaine is like est or Scientology," he figures. "It just allows you to be the asshole that you want to be."

By this time, Harry had returned to the live stage to great acclaim in what were best de-

scribed as one-man/performance art/multi-media presentations (parts of which were eventually filmed for a 1988 HBO special). Among other things, he included a dead-on impersonation of Michael Jackson dancing at a plastic surgery institute ("Because Hope Never Leaves a Scar"); a take-off on Los Angeles talk-show host Mr. Blackwell interviewing actor Bobby Boucher, who was starring in a revival of *Irma La Douce* at the James Franciscus Dinner Theater, who claimed to be the illegitimate offspring of Marilyn Monroe and President John F. Kennedy ("Oooooh," Shearer's Blackwell cooed to his guest, "I see Marilyn in your eyes—interesting!"); and finally, there was the book reading by the incredibly pompous Robert Bloom, the baseball writer for the *Atlantic Monthly* magazine, whose latest tome, *Not Since Noah*, chronicled "some of the more memorable rainouts I've experienced."

Finally, by 1990, Shearer was working on "The Simpsons," a few movies, his live shows, and his highly satirical radio programs, in an attempt to "translate my reputation into more visible work." And, the forty-seven year old vows, he'll keep at it until he reaches that goal. Right, a real eager beaver.

> *'I think cocaine is like est or Scientology. It just allows you to be the asshole that you want to be.'*

HARRY'S. . . . "New World Order" reggae

Sometimes you got to draw / a line in the sand. /

Sometimes you got to hit the ground / just like you planned. /

Your partners, whether they are common or royal /

Know that you're fighting / For so much more than oil./

Yeah, follow General Norm / As the shield turns to a storm. /

Someone's got to ride first class / Someone's got to be the porter./

Welcome, my friend / To the new world order. /

The new world order. /

Never before / Such a grand coalition./

United to change / The human condition./

Even though the Russians and the French / And the wacky Italians/

Keep lookin' for a way / To delay / The dashing battalions./

Hey, the war's already won. / Whooaaa, but the work's just begun./

Don't buy our arms then use them /

To cross your neighbor's border./ Oh, no./

Keep our arms at your side / That's the new world order./

Hey / The new world order./

Collateral damage / And a little friendly fire /

Are a small price to pay / For the future we require./

The rule of law / Used to sound so vague./

Until the troops came in / And they dispensed with The Hague./

Hey! / Whatever your belief. / Whooaa / Hail to the Chief!/

Uncle Sam just stands a little taller / 'Cause the rest of us are shorter./

Get in line my friends / For the new world order. / Hey! /

Any newsman in Baghdad / Must be a distorter. /

No news is good / In the new world order. / Hey! /

Take my word, every ward / Just needs a good warder. /

What else is new? / In the new world order./ Hey! /

The new world order. / The new world order.

Paula Poundstone was born in Alabama in 1960 but lived there only for a month before she figured she'd "done everything there was to do." In short, she bores easily. Still, she stayed at her next stop—the Boston suburb of Sudbury—a bit longer. But by the time she was eighteen years old, a high school dropout and decidedly estranged from her family, Paula Poundstone reckoned it was time to move on again. With that, she packed her bag and boarded a southbound bus heading for Florida in order to chase a much-cherished show-biz dream.

While she jokes on stage that "adults are always asking little kids what they want to be when they grow up because they're looking for ideas," at that time Poundstone definitely knew what she wanted to do. She wanted to become a bear in the Disney World parade.

"I went right to the casting department with my suitcase," she says matter-of-factly. "I would have taken any job, I suppose, but I really wanted to be a bear. And I was so specific that it really frightened them. I don't think people are prepared for someone who knows that firmly that they want to be a bear in the Disney World parade."

paula poundstone

Right she is, and the theme park's employment personnel passed on the opportunity to hire Poundstone. "Instead," she recalls, "I ended up working at the International House of Pancakes from eleven at night till seven in the morning, which wasn't exactly my second choice."

It was a short-lived interlude, however. A few months later, Paula was back in Boston waitressing at a salad bar restaurant ("I practically ran the place because I controlled the vegetables") and it was during that time that she first gave stand-up a shot. Even a brand new career, however, wasn't enough to keep her in one place. By the fall of 1980 she was back on a bus—this one heading west towards San Francisco. She fell in love with the city. In fact, Paula, who was once Robin Williams' roommate, now lives in Los Angeles, but she still maintains an apartment in San Francisco.

"In terms of the audience," she says of her first performance in 'Frisco, "it was like that scene in *The Wizard of Oz* when the house lands and it becomes technicolor. I worked the second or third night I was in town, and it was the most accepted I ever felt."

Since that time, Poundstone has been accepted by audiences all across the country (she spends about forty weeks a year on the club circuit), has made numerous appearances on "The Tonight Show" and "Late Night with David Letterman," and has already done a couple of solo specials for HBO.

Despite all of that, however, Paula has managed to remain incredibly insecure. Take, for instance, this observation: "I'm the kind of person salespeople won't come up to, security does." And though she admits to seeing her shrink "like every two minutes," that facet of her personality still comes as something of a surprise. It's especially surprising considering how confident she appears on stage and how warm, upbeat, and thoroughly candid she is in conversation—even when talking about the distance that still exists between her and her family.

"My mother called a couple of years ago," she recalls, "to complain that I make fun of her publicly. My father asked me to change my name. So they're pretty much bent out of shape right across the board. But I did tell them that I would change my first name to Jack—which is *his* name.

"I really don't have too much to do with them," she continues. "We just don't have enough in common that we seek each other out. But if we do, if there is ever like a death in the family," she concludes with a Cheshire smile, "I'm sure I'll be accused."

PAULA ON. . . .

Movies: You can't take anyone's word on a film. When *The Wizard of Oz* first came out it was badly reviewed. They said it was stupid and unimaginative. Isn't that amazing? What if it turns out that *Rambo 3* is really good?

Grooming: I happen to have weird hair which is why I don't dress up fancy. If I dress up, people just look at me and go, 'Oooh, look at her head.' This way here, it's more of a total look and nobody can put their finger on quite what they think is wrong.

Her mother: She used to get mad over absolutely everything. I remember the time I knocked a Flintstones glass off the table and she said, 'Damnit, that's why we can't have nice things.'

Working out with weights: If you have to lift something and it makes you go, 'Arrrrgggghhhh,' put that down!

'If you have to lift something and it makes you go, "Arrrrgggghhhh," put that down!'

Wishful thinking: One night I was in my house all by myself and all the lights went out. I go, 'There's a guy in the basement, he flipped a switch, he's coming up to kill me.' And then I realized the whole neighborhood was out and I was kinda relieved because I thought, 'Maybe he'll start at the end of the block.'

Culinary skills: I met some guy who told me he likes to eat chocolate-flavored Pop Tarts. He breaks them up, puts them into a bowl, pours milk over them, and then eats them. I said, 'Well, hell. You might as well cook.' If you're using more than three steps, you're cooking in my opinion.

Warren Hutcherson's a born liar. Okay, maybe that isn't quite fair. To be perfectly honest, he wasn't born a liar—but as he got older, he certainly got real good at it. Which, if truth be told, is absolutely fine by us.

"I take a couple of grains of truth," the Baltimore native says of his on-stage material, "and then I invent situations and embellish them a little."

A little? Well, judge for yourselves. Take, for instance, this wonderfully crafted bit, which helped him win the $50,000 grand prize in the 1990 Merit Comedy Contest.

He told the sold-out audience at Lincoln Center's Avery Fisher Hall that in 1969, his state trooper father joined the Nation of Islam and became a Muslim. It was something that the then-six-year-old Warren didn't exactly appreciate. "All of a sudden, I don't have a Christmas and I have to fast for a month." In the meantime, his born-again Christian grandmother, who was just as dazed

warren hutcherson

as he was, had a fit of pique (re-created by Warren on stage) and assured the child that he would indeed be privy to all the Yule season trimmings.

But, Hutcherson continued, the situation was further complicated by the fact that Grandma didn't know how to drive so the two had to rely on Dad to take them to the mall to visit Santa Claus—which was where a bad dream really turned into a nightmare.

"I finally get to the front of the line," he went on, "and Santa asked me, 'What do you want for Christmas?' And all of a sudden, I hear my Dad in the back of the room screaming, 'Tell him you want your FREEDOM! You got freedom in that bag, fat man?'

"All I was going to ask for," Warren concluded, to the audience's immense delight, "was maybe a G.I. Joe doll."

To set the record straight, though, that scene never really unfolded. To begin with, Dad was not a state trooper, but a laborer. What's more, while the elder Hutcherson, who passed away in 1982, had indeed joined the Nation of Islam in 1969 and was politically aware, he wasn't so jaded that he actually insisted that racist plots could be found in even the most absurd situations. ("Why," Warren mimics him on stage, "are the *green* olives in a jar but the *black* olives are locked in a can?")

Finally, to complete the dissection of Hutcherson's on-stage characterization of his father, the young Warren never really faced the possible loss of tinsel and wrapped treasures. His parents, you see, had separated four years earlier and he lived with his mother who had remained a Christian. Warren says now, "My father really was a Muslim. The rest of the stuff I invented. I mean," he laughs, "my father never threatened Santa Claus."

Well, it's comforting to know that Santa was spared such an unpleasant confrontation. Hutcherson, however, hasn't always been as lucky.

"One time in Baltimore," he remembers, "there was a Muslim in the audience. He didn't say anything to me after the show, but about a week later, he saw me on the bus and asked if I was a comic and if I had done a show a week earlier. I told him yes, and he said, 'Have you ever seen an asshole wrapped in plastic?' I said 'No,' and he said, 'Well, look at your license!'"

Pretty rough stuff—even for public transportation. But don't worry about this guy. Rest assured that Warren managed to get in the last word before he reached his stop. And that, ladies and gentlemen, is definitely on the level.

WARREN ON. . . .

Moving violations: I get stopped for speeding, but it's not my fault. It's the car's fault 'cause the car has 120 on the speedometer, and when you

pay a lot of money for something, you want to make sure it operates at its optimum level.

So I get mad at the police for even stopping me. 'Hey, I'm on 78, I'm trying to get to 120. If you would wait for me in the next state, I'll be there in five minutes. What the hell is wrong with you people?'

Copping a plea: I should be able to claim temporary insanity for speeding. I mean, I could kill somebody, go into court, and plead temporary insanity, and they would actually consider it. But they won't consider it for speeding, even though it makes more sense to say, 'Officer, I was doing the limit and then for five minutes I just went nuts! Thanks for stopping me.'

And if that's a real plea, you should be able to call in insane for work. Then you wouldn't have to waste your time with that little sick voice since they don't know how you sound when you're crazy. 'Hi, I can't come in today, I'm insane. No, it's a temporary thing. Yeah, twenty-four hours. I think I'll be back tomorrow.'

❝*You should be able to call in insane for work. Then you wouldn't have to waste your time with that little sick voice. "Hi, I can't come in today, I'm insane. No, it's a temporary thing. Yeah, twenty-four hours. I think I'll be back tomorrow."*❞

Richard Jeni will tell you that he never knew where his place was in this world. Sure, now he can get on stage with a cool, confident swagger and talk about anything he chooses. But, he insists, there was a time when he felt like a definite outsider. In fact, he's had this feeling since he was quite small, and claims that his birth by caesarian section was "the last time I had my mother's complete attention."

"I was too much of a street kid to hang out with the student government/football people," the Brooklyn native remembers, "but not enough of an idiot to be with the drugged-out, 'let's-beat-up-the-other-people' guys. I was kind of a free agent—a man without a clique in high school. Always. Never had a place to fit in. So I'd pretend to be in either of those groups when I was with them."

Still, despite his social duplicity—or perhaps, because of it—Richard somehow made it through high school and New York's Hunter College. He even maintained a 3.9 grade point average along the way and graduated with honors. His feelings of being out of step with the rest of the world, however, followed him well past his academic years.

"When I got out of college and got into the business world," Jeni says with a shrug, "I didn't fit in there, either. My problem was I didn't want to take orders and I didn't want to be the boss—and those are about the only two jobs they've got.

"Every job I ever had I was a complete fuck-up in," continues Richard, who points out that he was fired from five jobs in two years. "I was an unmitigated disaster because I can't do anything unless it's my idea—even if it makes sense.

"And that," he says, "is how I got into this business—which is how I think most people wind up in show business. It's not like you're a surgeon and then, one day in the middle of an operation you go, 'Hey, I should go to a nightclub and talk about my penis in public.' Usually, you're headed down the rapids and the falls are coming up and there's this branch—*comedy!*—and *whomp!*—you hold on."

That limb first appeared in 1981, at an open-mike audition, and after having a few shots of liquid courage, he grabbed it. And Jeni (whose early material included the line, "The name Agnes Moorehead sounds like a request") held on tight—despite the fact that the money was bad, the rooms were worse, and his act had, shall we say, a minimalist feel to it.

"I didn't have a lot of material back then," Richard says with a laugh. "I used to pad it with what were the longest segues known to man. People would say to me, 'Hey, you've got some good jokes, why don't you shorten the segues?' And I'd tell them, 'If I shortened the segues, I'd have seven minutes of act.'

But things do change. Jeni, who now lives in Los Angeles and who has more than a decade's worth of material stored in the recesses of his brain, could probably stage a two-and-a-half hour show consisting mainly of his tried and true hits. (Like his idea that Chicago got started by a bunch of New Yorkers who said, "Gee, I'm enjoying the crime and poverty but it just isn't cold enough.") And, he assures us, all of his material is there for one reason—to entertain, not lecture.

"Comedians," he believes, "don't lead anybody into battle. Comedians, ultimately, even the biggest ones, don't make a difference. What they *can* do is be in the USO and make everybody forget about the charge for a little while. That's where I see the value in what I do. I don't see myself changing anybody's life. I see myself as giving people a break."

RICHARD ON. . . .

Whether to tie the knot: Married or single—it's a choice you have to make. Sort of like a doctor asking you if you want ointment or suppository.

richard jeni

Connubial bliss: Half of all marriages end in divorce. The other half end in death. Who knows? You could be one of the lucky ones.

Personal questions: People ask me, 'Do you have kids?' Whoa! I don't even have real houseplants—back off!

Video rentals: I've never been disappointed by an X-rated movie. You never say, 'Gee, I didn't think it would end that way!'

Childhood memories: They told me in school to have a hot breakfast.

My mother said, 'Hot breakfast? Ha! Swallow some water in the shower.'

Being a man: I got into a fight in the South. Well, it really wasn't a fight—he hit me and I fell down. Still, I felt like I participated.

Statistics: They found out that ninety percent of men masturbated. The other ten percent? No arms!

Sex surveys: Who's going to tell the truth about their sexual life to a guy who shows up at ten in the morning with a clipboard?

'Ding, dong,' you open the door in your bathrobe. . . .

'Excuse me, sir, do you jerk off?'

'That's pretty rough talk for a Jehovah's Witness, isn't it?'

> *Chicago got started by a bunch of New Yorkers who said, "Gee, I'm enjoying the crime and poverty but it just isn't cold enough."*

It's no shock to learn that Joy Behar is from Brooklyn. Even if she didn't tell you, that voice would be a dead giveaway. It's throaty, no-nonsense, and sounds like its owner was cracking gum and standing on Flatbush Avenue just minutes ago. And *marone*, the things that she says with it!

"My mother always said to me, 'Good luck with your mouth!'" Joy Behar remembers with a rather hearty laugh. "I always got into trouble with the things I said out of turn. I just didn't know my place."

Well, even if she didn't know it then, she certainly found it. And if the quest took her longer than it should have, the trek seemed preordained. After all, this self-proclaimed "blabbermouth" figures, her urge to take center-stage was in the genes.

Joy, an Italian-American woman who was born Josephine Occhiuto, reports that "my mother was a frustrated performer. When I was a kid she'd get up and sing and I'd go right under the table. Oh!" she shudders, "I used to get soooo embarrassed!"

Eventually Behar got over those feelings, but being embarrassed by a parent runs in the family. "I've never been embarrassed by anything she has done on stage," Behar's grown daughter Eve says of her mother. "I only get embarrassed in real life sometimes—like if she has a fight with a saleslady, or something."

Always having trouble with the mouth, that one. Still, at least Joy's putting it to good use these days (in addition to stand-up and TV appearances, she hosts a morning talk-radio show in New York). But that wasn't always the case.

After graduating from Queens College with a master's degree in English, Behar tried her hand at being a happy homemaker. ("I was married to a Spanish Jew. We used to worship at the Temple Julio Iglesias."), a phase she says, that lasted "for about ten minutes." From there, it was on to short-lived careers as an employment counselor for the state and as an instructor in a hospital for the mentally impaired.

Joy followed those jobs with a lengthy stretch as a public school teacher and left that after five years because "it was just too hard." No wonder—she was teaching remedial English to tough kids in a rough neighborhood in the Bronx.

"These were the kind of kids," she jokes, "who would set fire to their parents and then they'd be sent to me to teach them the difference between 'who' and 'whom.' I tried to make it relevant. I'd say, '*Whom* do you wish to kill? Not who!'"

Finally, in 1979, she broke into show business. Or, more specifically, she broke in *front* of show business when she was hired as a receptionist for "Good Morning America." As one would suspect, office work didn't prove to be her forte.

"It took me a year to get promoted from receptionist to secretary," the fortyish divorcée remembers with a laugh. "Other people did it in two months! And I had a master's degree, mind you!

"Why?" she asks rhetorically. "Because I'm a blabbermouth—which is probably the same reason I got fired."

It was 1983 at that point, and she was finally ready to take those first steps into the spotlight. Of course everybody thought she was crazy but, hey, as Behar figured, screw 'em.

"I like comedy," she says with a shrug and a wide smile. "I guess it's because this is a job without a net. It's funny—when I was a housewife, I was going crazy. It was too safe. I don't know what it is, but I'm just one of those people who doesn't feel safe in safe situations."

JOY ON. . . .

Companionship: I'm at a point where I want a man in my life—but not in my house! Just come in, attach the VCR, and get out.

j o y   b e h a r

Her mother: The woman thought the movie *Deep Throat* was the life story of Luciano Pavarotti.

Italians and traveling: These are not the Vikings we're talking about. They make the big trip from Calabria, they go to Avenue Z in Brooklyn, and they stay there for fifty years.

The gals who administer bikini waxes: These women studied at the Klaus Barbie School of Beauty in Dusseldorf.

Heather Locklear: Does she still have that commercial running? Where she comes out in that little string bikini? She comes out and says, 'Are you ready for the competition?'—*I'll smack her!* It's like, shut up, Heather! Go do something with your life! Go teach the handicapped, go save the whales, take care of the homeless, *get off my back!*

‘*I'm at a point where I want a man in my life—but not in my house! Just come in, attach the VCR, and get out.*’

Air travel: My mother told me, 'Don't be afraid of flying because when it's your turn to die, you'll die. *Que sera, sera.*' The woman studied with St. Augustine and Doris Day. I told her, 'Ma, what if I'm on the plane and it's the pilot's time to die?'

Celebrity perfumes: Cher has a fragrance out. And on her commercial she says, 'I call it Uninhibited because there are so many people inside of me.' Yeah—and they're all under eighteen.

Sam Kinison had already made a huge splash in Los Angeles and now the controversial comedian was making his New York headlining debut at Caroline's Comedy Club. It was January 1986, and the room on that Tuesday night was packed with the people that mattered. Finally he took the stage and over the course of the next ninety minutes or so, Kinison ranted and raved like a hellfire-and-brimstone preacher.

Among other things, he wondered about the problem of starvation in Africa. What do we do to help? he inquired. We give them things like sacks of flour and wheat. What good is that, he pointed out—after all, if somebody dropped a bag of wheat at his feet he wouldn't "know what the fuck to do with it either." Besides, he went on, many of these poor souls were living in the desert—so instead of bringing in truckloads of food, why don't we go in with empty trucks, load them up with these starving hordes, and "bring *them* to where the food is!"

Most of the audience was stunned by the energy of this gnome-like presence who stalked the stage wearing a dark overcoat and beret. Some, however, were stung by his act. After a particularly vicious harangue against his two ex-wives, which, of course, concluded with his trademark scream ("If you ever get married I want you to remember this face—*Oh! Oooooooooohhhhhh!*"), a couple of women in the audience left the club in a huff. As the show went on, a few others followed suit. Still, by and large, Kinison scored big-time that night.

Afterwards, Kinison was basking in the adoration being showered on him when somebody suggested that they all go to another club, where boxing promoter Don King was throwing a party for Pia Zadora. Great idea. So Sam got his entourage together—which included his fur-draped mother, a minister's wife from Tulsa, Ok-lahoma, who'd travelled East for her son's big opening night.

It was at the Pia "do" where Sam Kinison's real impact on people came to the forefront. During a quiet moment, someone asked his mom if, in fact, Sam had really been a minister in his younger years. "Oh, yes," she twanged, with a wide smile. "Sam was touched by the hand of God."

"Really?" muttered a woman who'd seen his show earlier that evening. "That hand should have come down and smacked him across the fucking face."

"Some people," Sam's mother said, looking somewhat pained, "just don't get him."

Would those include members of her husband's congregation?

"I suppose," she answered. "But he just tells them, 'I've been praying for your children for years. Now it's time for you to pray for one of mine.'"

sam kinison

In the years following that night, Sam has definitely given them cause to hit their knees. Critics have savaged him, calling him sexist and homophobic. In 1988, *Atuk*, which would have been the first movie that Sam starred in, closed one day into production amid rumors of scandal and lawsuits. That same year, there was his well-publicized friendship with ministerial groupie Jessica Hahn, followed by an equally well-publicized divorce from his wife, Terry, a year later. Too, there was the time a distraught Sam called New York radio dee-jay Howard Stern and made the painfully shocking announcement that one of the Kinison brothers had just taken his own life. And through it all, there was all that cocaine and booze.

Finally, in 1990, he claimed that he'd cleaned up his act. "I had a dangerous problem," he said at the time, "but at least I stopped before I lost everything."

But it should be pointed out that for Kinison, sobriety didn't mean cleaning up his on-stage

act. In 1990 he released an album called *Leader of the Banned*. Aside from its contents, the cover caused a furor because it featured the former minister surrounded by a gaggle of scantily clad women in a parody of the "Last Supper." Once again, Some people just didn't get it—despite his recorded insistence that he was "Mr. Family Entertainment."

There are some churchgoers in Tulsa, no doubt, who figure he must have been referring to the Manson family.

SAM ON. . . .

Sexual counseling: Dr. Ruth can spiel her wrinkled elephant gray grandma-ass bullshit . . . but *I'm* outta line. . . . Where does she come from? There's a Haagen-Dazs somewhere missing a night manager. . . . I listened to her one day on the radio, she goes, 'Take the man's penis . . .' When was the last time she saw a fuckin' man's penis? . . . Who was president then? . . . Were there cars then or did you suck dick on horseback, Annie Oakley? . . . She goes, 'If the man's penis is too small to satisfy the woman then it's perfectly acceptable for the woman to use a dildo or a vibrator and pleasure herself later after she has pleasured the man.' Oh, yeah, that's gonna give the marriage a second chance; that's gonna pump the guy full of sexual confidence. Here you are trying to make love to your wife and Mr. Tonka-toy over here would like a shot at it, all right? 'You want to plug me in on your way out of the bedroom. . . . Let's go! Move it!' *Rrrr-rrr-rr-rr-r!* 'I hope the grinding noise doesn't disturb "Miami Vice."'

Thanks to Dr. Ruth my wife's fuckin' a lawnmower.

Animal counseling: Dog psychiatry—I'd like to get in on some of that cash. Guy comin' into the fuckin' psychiatrist: 'It's Rusty, man. I don't know,

he used to be a sparky dog. He was a happy dude. And he used to play with the frisbee. And I don't know, he just hasn't been himself lately. He's losing his identity.'

'Yeah, come on in, Rusty, this way Rusty, yeah come on in. We'll go in and have a session. Yeah come on in Rusty, this way.'

'You're a fuckin' dog!' *Whomp!* 'You understand that?! You sit in the fuckin' yard!' *Whomp!* 'You bark! Bark! Bark, you sucker!'

'Yeah, listen, Rusty's all better now. Yeah, we had a real good session. That'll be two hundred bucks. Yeah, he's really opened up. He's found himself. Yeah, he's a new dog now.'

> ❝Dr. Ruth says, "If the man's penis is too small to satisfy the woman then it's perfectly acceptable for the woman to pleasure herself later after she has pleasured the man." Thank's to her my wife's fuckin' a lawnmower.❞

When Rita Rudner decided to try stand-up comedy, nobody was more surprised to hear that than her friends. Even though she had sung and danced her way through six Broadway shows and had made a number of television commercials at that point, they'd never expected the quiet Miami native to go such a personal and expressive route.

"My dancer friends," Rudner reported years later, "say I was never funny. They say I used to say two things a month that were witty—maybe—but other than that I didn't even talk much."

So it wasn't a surprising reaction at all, considering that even Rita calls herself a shy person. Rudner, who kids that her bright but easily distracted father would "throw me up in the air and go answer the phone," traces the roots of her shyness to her formative years. She started first grade at four-and-a-half years old, took eleventh and twelfth grades in one year, attended a couple of summer courses along the way, and graduated high school at the very tender age of sweet sixteen.

"Since I was always younger than everyone else," she says, "I didn't talk very much because I was afraid to say the wrong thing. So I listened a lot. And that actually helped me because I think comedians should be good listeners, not good talkers necessarily. A good comedian" she concludes "doesn't have to be the life of the party."

A good comedian does, however, have to be prepared. And by 1980, when Rudner passed her first audition at New York's Improvisation, she was ready. A fan of Woody Allen and Jack Benny, she recalls that "every day I went to the library and got as many books and records about comedy as I could. I would go to the Museum of Broadcasting and look at old shows. I did my own little comedy course. I studied every day. I worked for months on that first five minutes of material. A lot of people," she concludes, "approached comedy as a lark. Not me."

The discipline paid off indeed. And despite the fact that Rita insists that "I'm at least ten years behind schedule in all areas of my life," she has never regretted her career switch—not even at the beginning.

"When I tried it for the first time," she says, "I loved it; otherwise I never would have done it. It was too hard. I didn't know how hard it was. I thought I'd write six jokes and everything would be fine. I really didn't know what I was in for. But then, I figure, if people knew what they were in for in life, they wouldn't even go out."

Rita, on the other hand, always sallied forth—both professionally and personally. And it was the latter, incidentally, that played a large part in her act. Through the years, to hear Rudner tell it on stage, life was just one achingly funny romantic mishap after another ("I broke up with my boyfriend because he wanted to get married. I didn't want him to"). Since she was so identified with her single status, comedy insiders worried that a happy, permanent relationship would ruin her career.

Still, despite her joke that she would look at potential mates and wonder "Is this the man I want my children to spend their weekends with?" Rudner bit the bullet and married British TV producer Martin Bergman in 1988—albeit, with at least one reservation. "That's a big question a comedienne has to ask herself before she gets married," says Rudner with a little smile. "'Am I willing to give up twenty minutes worth of material for this man?'"

Again, Rita is happy with her choice. "For him," she reports with an even wider smile, "I would have given up forty minutes."

rita rudner

Jerry Seinfeld's apartments in Los Angeles and New York, apparently, are furnished in what would best be termed as Spartan motif. Jay Leno, in fact, once cracked that Jerry Seinfeld's West Coast digs looked "like a hospital with a stereo."

"I like things very spare," Jerry says in defense of his choice of decor. "I like to keep my mind uncluttered. I'm leaving home every other day so I don't want to leave any place that is too cozy. This way, I can look around and think, 'I'm really glad to be getting the hell out of here!'"

And where he's going is to work. When not busy with his TV series, "Seinfeld," he tours. Not that he needs to; it's just that he *needs* to.

"Comedy," he explains, "is like an athletic experience. If you take a few nights off, you can feel you've lost half a step. If I don't work all the time, I don't feel that I'm in control of it."

The man is, as he readily admits, "a joke-aholic"—which is just the way the non-drinker, non-smoker prefers it. "To me, my whole life is a vacation. I make more money and I have more fun when I'm working than when I'm not working. I'm paid to joke around."

And the jokes he makes the rounds with are mostly witty observations on the travails of modern life, put forth with a thoroughly friendly, rather low-key delivery. "What I do best," he says, "is concentrate on the little, mundane moments in life." These can run from his inability to grasp why water ruins suede ("Do the cows knock on the farmer's door when it rains? 'Let us in—we're all wearing leather!'") to giving voice to the sock that's always missing after the laundry is finished (the one that plotted its escape in the hamper the night before).

It is a tactic, incidentally, that has changed little since Steinfeld first started doing comedy in 1978 when he was fresh out of college. Jerry, you see, who has a strong interest in Zen philosophy and puts himself through a taxing ninety-minute daily Yoga workout. And he is definitely a purist on stage as well—no props, no characters, no swearing, no axe to grind. In short, it's no-frills comedy, as close to perfection as possible.

But near-perfection can take a few years to achieve and Seinfeld is still working at it. "I aspire to improving as a stand-up comic," he says. "No one has ever been *too* good at it."

This guy knows whereof he speaks; even *he* wasn't always so confident on stage. There was, for instance, his first road gig, when he found himself in an upstate New York resort hotel facing a roomful of people who were, at best, middle-aged.

"I was twenty-two and I had no material that was vaguely appropriate for these people," he remembers with a little laugh. "And I was wearing, like, my bar mitzvah suit with the short pants.

jerry seinfeld

"All I had to do," he continues, "was fifteen minutes and I couldn't do it. It was grisly. The booking agent came up to me after the show and told me I might be in for a rough career—that people may not understand me in America."

Amazing how much this country has changed since then, huh?

JERRY ON. . . .

The need to impress: Why does McDonald's have to count every burger that they sell? What is their ultimate goal? Do they want cows surrendering voluntarily? . . . They should just put up signs: 'MacDonald's—We're Doing *Very* Well.'

Strange road signs: What about that one that says 'Left turn, okay'? It's like, 'We're not *crazy* about you turning here but if you have to, well, *okay*.'

Legal addresses: My parents live in Florida now. They didn't want to move there but they're over sixty, and it's the law.

Home decoration: My mother insists that a mir-

rored wall gives the illusion of more space. Like some jerk is going to walk up to a mirror and say, 'Hey, there's a whole other room in there just like this one. And there's a guy in there who looks just like me'. . . My mother had a parakeet who used to fly around the house and would smack right into the mirror. Even if he thought it was another room you'd think he'd at least try to avoid hitting the other parakeet.

'My parents live in Florida now. They didn't want to move there but they're over sixty, and it's the law.'

It can be a real thankless job. After all, the audience is definitely not there to see Angela Scott. They want to see Bill or Phylicia or Malcolm or any of the other regulars. That's why they left work early. That's the whole point here.

So, they want to know, who is *that* woman with the mike? Meet Angela Scott, the woman who warms up the audience for "The Cosby Show." *That* woman with the mike down there.

Backstage, some two hours after the audience has first arrived, Scott says, "People don't realize how long it takes to tape a show. They think it's half an hour, they think they can kick back and then go out to dinner. But I have to keep them up and not thinking about food or about leaving.

"And I really do try to keep the food jokes to a minimum," she continues with a little shake of her head. "But it's awfully difficult sometimes. Like one week they had a barbecue on the show and the smell of chicken is wafting up to the audience. I thought they were going to stampede—and I *knew* they wanted to kill me at any moment."

It can be a tough gig, but somebody has got to do it. And this divorced mother of two grown children is happy to be that somebody. After four years of being on "Cosby"'s off-camera payroll, Angela reports, "I'm not being schmaltzy, but every time I come here I still get a tingle."

Part of that, no doubt, is the challenge of facing a tough audience—which is something she *knows* from. Back in the late '60s, while a student at Harvard, Scott embraced a political philosophy that was considered a little, er, radical at the time. How radical? Well, take this bit from her act:

"I met my husband in college," she tells the audience. "We were politically active—a little militant."

Pause.

"We were Black Panthers. They said have babies for the revolution. And I'm *still* miffed with the Panther Party because nobody told *me* that they weren't going to babysit."

"I watch people die when I say that," says Scott off stage. "They don't believe me."

While comics have been known to make up a thing or two in order to get a laugh, that bit is truly a slice of Angela's life. It was an episode that began in 1968, and it lasted for two-and-a-half years. It was a time of political and social upheaval and Scott, who was born in New York and raised in the middle-class community of Concord, Massachusetts, was decidedly in the thick of things.

And she definitely looked the part—outfitted, as she was, with her infant son Peter in one arm and an unloaded 30.06 rifle in the other. It was a fashion ensemble that definitely caused something of a stir. While people didn't have a problem with the baby, many found her other accessory a little hard to take.

angela scott

"They actually asked me to leave school because I wanted to bring my rifle into class with me. *Imagine!*" she says with mock, wide-eyed disbelief.

In time she had a second child (daughter Erica), left the Panther Party, and moved back to New York. Once there, she "all of a sudden got this acting bug" and successfully auditioned for the Negro Ensemble Theater's workshops. From there she joined a black comedy team (whose ranks included filmmaker Robert Townsend), and finally, she took a solo flight on the stand-up stage in 1982.

While her life has followed a rather circuitous path, the message has remained the same—only the tactics have changed. "I feel good about what I did at the time because it was needed at that time. But now," she insists, "I'm a total pacifist. There has got to be another way. A dialogue has got to happen."

Scott's keeping up her end of the conversation—on stage and armed with wit. And this time around, her weapon is loaded.

ANGELA ON. . . .

Aging gracefully: When I tell people that I have a son who is twenty-three and a daughter who is twenty they say, 'You know, you can never tell how old you people are. You could live forever.' Yeah, if I don't get stopped for speeding.

School daze: I grew up in Concord, Massachusetts, and we were the only black family there. So, you know how when a subject comes up that may include you people tend to stare at you? Well, whenever they'd talk about Africa when I was in school, everyone would turn around and stare at me like I suddenly got a spear in my hand.

> *The first person to die during the American Revolutionary War was a black man, Crispus Attucks. They said, "Go see if you see anybody with guns." BOOM! . . . "Guess they had guns."*

American history: The first person to die during the American Revolutionary War was a black man, Crispus Attucks. They said, 'Go see if you see anybody with guns.' BOOM! 'Guess they had guns.'

Different perspectives: Southerners are very friendly people. I won't go on a picnic at night with them, but that's just me. Now 125 years later, they still don't admit to losing the Civil War. However, they admit to misplacing it.

Let's just say that Larry Miller has gotten lucky in Las Vegas a couple of times—not necessarily at the casino tables, but lucky nonetheless. He went, he saw, he met two of his heroes. And Larry remembers both introductions like they happened yesterday.

The first time around, he wasn't alone. He and his good friend Jerry Seinfeld were both off for a couple of days when they found out that Bill Cosby was performing in Las Vegas. The two were just starting to make a little headway in the business, and as far as they were concerned, Cosby was the greatest. So, like the ardent fans they were, they boarded a plane in New York City and headed west to that desert city. "We just wanted to see him perform," Miller says.

Once there, however, they decided they wanted more. After all, they figured, they came all this way, they were comics just like their idol, and the least they could do was let Cosby know that they were in

larry miller

town. But after they found the nerve to call his room, they got a terrific shock. Rather than telling them to buzz off, Cosby actually invited them up for a chat.

"When we were standing in the lobby," Larry recalls with a laugh, "we must have looked like a couple of nine year olds hoping to see Babe Ruth or something. We might as well have been wearing little caps on the side of our heads and carrying old, beat-up baseball gloves."

To hear Miller tell it today, however, it was even better than meeting the Babe could possibly have been. "He told us to come up, and he talked to us for three hours before the show. And then he talked to us again *after* the show.

"It was a truly lovely day," concludes Larry. "We were not only blown away by the show, but we left there thinking, 'Now, *there's* a guy.'"

The second of his landmark Vegas meetings was even better. Not only did Miller, whose impeccably written yarns include one near classic, "The Five Levels of Drinking" (beginning with "I can still get seven hours of sleep" and ending well beyond "I know! I'll stay up all night"), get to shake hands with Frank Sinatra, he also got paid for the privilege.

Ol' Blue Eyes, apparently, needed a comic to open a week of his shows. His daughter, Tina, who had seen Miller perform at an L.A. charity benefit, suggested that her father hire the Long Island native. He did—and only with a few days notice.

So Miller, who was featured as the clothing store salesmen in the hit movie, "Pretty Woman," arrived the same day as his first show and had just enough time to check into the hotel and make his way down to the dressing room to get ready for his performance. As he began getting out of his street clothes, someone from Sinatra's entourage knocked on his dressing room door and said that Frank would like to come by in a couple of minutes to meet him. Miller said, "fine," and continued dressing. By the time he had his shirt on and was pulling up his tuxedo pants, the door flung open and in walked Sinatra.

"When I went to shake his hand," Larry recalls with a laugh, "my pants dropped to my ankles."

And because Miller didn't want to interrupt this moment, the pants stayed where they fell the whole time the two chatted. "He was very cool," says Miller, "he didn't say a word about it."

Finally, Sinatra headed for the door, Larry bent down for his pants, Sinatra turned back at the last moment and Miller dropped his drawers once more. "Sinatra told me," says Miller, "'If that's in your act, kid, I hope you close with it.'

LARRY ON. . . .

Sexual attraction: Women are like the most powerful magnet in the universe. And all men are like cheap metal.

The softening of America: My father used to work three jobs and then go to night school. If I go to the cleaners and the bank in the same day, I need a nap. . . . By the time he was my age, my father had served in the war, built a house, raised a family. My greatest accomplishment so far is having all five 'Planet of the Apes' films on tape.

Breaking up is hard to do: I just broke up with someone and the last thing she said to me was, 'You'll never find anyone else like me again!' I'm thinking, 'I should hope not!' . . . 'If I don't want you, why would I want someone just like you?'

Short cuts: A friend of mine runs in marathons. He's always talking about this 'runner's high, 'but he has to go 26 miles for it. That's why I smoke and drink. I can get the same sensation by climbing a flight of stairs.

Leering techniques: Women say, 'Oh, we look at men sexually, too.'. . . Ladies, you have no idea. . . . It's the difference between shooting a bullet and throwing it.

The dangers of aging: You become 21, you turn 30, you're pushing 40, you reach 50, you make it to 60—and then you've built up so much speed, you HIT 70. After that, it's day by day. You hit Wednesday. . . .

'My father used to work three jobs and then go to night school. If I go to the cleaners and the bank in the same day, I need a nap.'

There are no one-liners in Bob Nelson's act. Instead, there is a dizzying array of character pieces. To paraphrase that popular saying, he's got so many characters, so little stage time.

In the course of a ninety-minute show, however, he's likely to bring out at least four or five of his favorites, like Jiffy Jeff, a punch-drunk ex-fighter who now runs a boxing school and who, for lack of a better expression, hears bells that ain't ringing; or the farmer and the duck bit, which he introduces as "a pantomime piece with sound effects and I talk during it." There's even an entire all-star college football team that he parades in front of the mike (which includes the fey "Bruce Koskiovsky, San Francisco University, tight end—next year I hope to be a wide receiver").

And there's more. Take the nerdy Eppie Epperman who blows bubbles into the air, and then runs around sucking the bubbles back into his mouth, doing an imitation of fish having dinner. Or there's the professional football player who screws up a commercial for the United Way by uttering lines like "If I did not play football I would not be playing football today" and "A mind is a terrible thing." And there's the drunk in the bar who takes a sip from his drink, drools all over himself and apologizes with, "I'm sorry, I must be full." And there's the Greek fisherman. And the old man, Grandpa Stone. And the Israeli guy. And Ping Yeh, the Chinese guy. . . .

And, well, you must get the picture by now.

"I sort of get immersed in my characters," says Nelson.

Talk about your understatements. These guys are very real to Bob. Real enough that he laments that "I'll create a routine and I'll end up giving it to Jiffy Jeff or to Eppie when I really should be doing it myself," and they're real enough to have taken part in his 1987 wedding.

bob nelson

"On the invitations we had 'Grandpa Stone, Eppie Epperman, and Ping Yeh request the honor of your presence at the marriage of their friends Patricia Ann O'Connor and Mr. Bob Nelson.' Everybody on Patty's side of the family," he remembers with a chuckle, "wanted to know who those people were."

In fact, those people have brought Nelson from his native Massapequa, Long Island, to stages all over the country, to television specials and even to featured roles in movies. Well, he's gotten a little help from Rodney Dangerfield, who can't claim that he gets no respect from Nelson. "Nobody," says Bob, "has helped me as much as he has. He's almost like a relative—the uncle in the business that I never had."

As for his real relatives, the vote was split. While his mother was behind him all the way, his construction worker father had definite reservations about Bob's career choice.

"My father," he says, "hated me doing comedy. He thought it was the worst thing I could do—until I did the 'Merv Griffin Show.' Then he became my biggest fan. And he still is."

Even though Dad was reticent at the beginning, Nelson had other people in his corner. One of these, a promoter named King Broder, hit on the idea of packaging three young comics together on one show and booking them into clubs. He called his creation the Identical Triplets and hired Nelson, Jim Meyers (who was eventually replaced by Rob Bartlett), and a very young Eddie Murphy.

Nelson, who auditioned for "Saturday Night Live" the same time as Murphy, is still in touch with Meyers and Bartlett, but over the last few years, he's lost contact with Murphy. "At one point," he remembers, "we were collaborating on a movie called *Satan's Key*. We stopped working together and to this day I don't know why. I mean we were writing a movie together one day and the next day his number was changed.

"He used to call me 'The Coach,'" says Bob with a grin, "because I would go out with him and all of his friends and it would be like all these black guys and me. Eddie said it looked like they were a basketball team and I looked like the coach."

Well, even if the friendship isn't rekindled, Nelson can still put together a team. Hell, he's got enough people in his head for that already.

BOB ON. . . .

The New York attitude towards personal injury: New Yorkers are the only ones who'll laugh at that, just New Yorkers. Down South they don't think like that. New York is a whole different story. It's like, 'Holy shit, he almost took his eye out! Y'know something, I haven't laughed this hard since I saw that fat guy slip on the ice outside.'

'A drunk in a bar takes a sip from his drink, drools all over himself, and says, 'I'm sorry, I must be full.'

Funniest thing I ever saw: I'm walking through the mall, my wife and kids, we were walkin' down the mall. They're puttin' up the glass doors, they're closin' the fuckin' mall, all right? This guy doesn't see the doors are goin' up. He's goin' right for the glass. My wife says, 'Omigod! You better tell him he's gonna hit the glass.' I said, *Shut the fuck up!* (I think this is gonna be funny, personally. Y'know what I'm sayin'?)

All of a sudden he runs right into the glass. BOOM! He hit it. It *was* funny. His face looked like rubber, I swear. It was like three times his head bounced off: Ba-ba-ba-boom! Like that, y'know?

And he's bleedin', he's layin' on the ground, he's cryin'. I'm laughin' my ass off! I couldn't help it. But I did, I called an ambulance. I had to. I couldn't breathe. I thought I was gonna pass out.

His network series' debut was just days away and Kevin Meaney was feeling quite playful. After all, here he was, sitting in a huge, borrowed New York office that some TV executive had vacated for the day; assistants were running around bringing him anything he needed; and all these people from the press wanted to talk to him. In short, it seemed like everybody at CBS that morning in the fall of 1990 was treating him like the star they hoped "Uncle Buck" would make him.

It was indeed a heady time for Kevin. So, when the phone on the impressive, polished desk rang—once, twice, and then three and four times—and the secretary stationed in the outer office seemed to be otherwise engaged, it was little surprise that Meaney picked up the receiver with an exaggerated flourish and officiously announced, "CBS." After all, what else is a comic to do when he is faced with an unexpected prop? What else, indeed, but play out the scene for all it's worth.

kevin meaney

"CBS," he repeated to his hapless victim, "can I help you? This is Brent Mussberger."

"That's right," he continued to the ever more confused caller, "this is CBS."

The exchange lasted only for a minute or so before the returning secretary desperately intercepted the call. Still, Meaney managed to hang on long enough to inform whoever it was on the other end of the line that, "I have a tie on and a suit on but I'm not wearing any underwear!"

Based on this episode it was no wonder that, as he insists in his act, his mother constantly called him "a *craaaaazy* person" and feared that his antics would ultimately cause the family "to lose the house." But there is further proof to substantiate that charge.

During a single conversation with Kevin on this particular day, he takes on the personalities of his nosy California landlady, Johnny Carson,

a psychotically perky morning talk show host, his mother, an insulting Southern newspaper reporter and even "Buck" co-star Audrey Meadows. And those are only the ones that we remember—there definitely could have been more. In other words, with all of those different people swirling around in his head, there's almost no talking to the *real* guy these days.

In fact, Meaney's parents had also wondered who they were talking to when he left his steady gig as a night manager for the airline catering service Sky Chef in order to pursue a career in comedy. "We were nervous at the beginning," says his mother, Patricia. "He had a good job at that time and comedy just didn't seem stable."

Well, neither did Kevin. And his parents' feelings of dread only escalated when Meaney, in some of his funniest on-stage bits, would all of a sudden be possessed by the character of his mother—a woman he presents as a shrill, whining nag forever on his case. While the audience may have been laughing, however, Mother Meaney, who describes herself as a "very shy person," was not always amused.

"In the beginning," she recalls, "it bothered me a little when he talked about me, but now I think he's very funny and it doesn't bother me anymore. Now I just say to him, 'Why don't you talk about Dad once in a while?' And he says someday he will."

Not that this is some sort of altruistic gesture. Mrs. Meaney, it should be pointed out, wasn't necessarily feeling bad because Dad was being left out of the act. "To be honest," she concludes with a giggle, "I just wanted the heat off."

We can only hope there's little chance of that.

KEVIN (and his mother) ON. . . .

Staying in shape: I've been doing the Fonda workout: the Peter Fonda workout. That's where I wake up, take a hit of acid, smoke a joint, and go over to my sister's house and ask her for money.

Avoiding accidents: Anything in my house could poke an eye out when I was a kid—even passing a piece of pizza. *You're gonna take your brother's eye out with that slice! Now put your goggles on and go to bed!*

Correct attire: We couldn't wear tight pants in my family. *Why are you wearing those tight pants? Going outside with tight pants on—you're like a craaaaaazy person! We're big pants people. Now go upstairs and put on your big pants. The Lobermans are coming over. Your father doesn't wear tight pants! STOP IT! Your brother doesn't wear tight pants! STOP IT!! Get that knife out of your hand! Coming at your mother with a knife—you're going to take my eye out! Why do you do this to us?*

Fast food: I almost got into a fight at Jack in the Box the other night. I went in and ordered a hamburger and the woman behind the counter asked me if I wanted any Jack sauce. I said, 'Jack sauce? Exactly what is Jack sauce, ma'am?' She tells me it's a secret. I said, 'No, thanks. You can hold the Jack sauce.' Some guy comes out of the back and says 'I make the Jack sauce!'

Why do you do things like that? Making Jack sauce? That's not right! One way or the other you are going to lose your sight!

> **❛*I've been doing the Fonda workout: the Peter Fonda workout. That's where I wake up, take a hit of acid, smoke a joint, and go over to my sister's house and ask her for money.*❜**

Let's get one thing straight right off. Steve Mittleman, who's been doing stand-up since 1977, doesn't have a lot of bad nights on stage. Most of them, in fact, are really quite good. It's just that the less-than-great ones have a tendency to stick in his mind.

Take, for instance, one of his first gigs in the late '70s. It was at a swim club in New York, he was to be paid $200 ("a big deal back then"), but he had to perform poolside, and the sound system was so bad it could only be heard halfway across the room. Making matters worse, a belly dancer suffering from the stomach flu (!) was opening the show for him. Somehow she got through her act and Mittleman, who was "supposed to do forty-five minutes and was "terrified," waited for his introduction. At last it came.

"And now," the emcee announced, "David Letterman."

Mittleman, who was off stage, shouted out a correction.

"And now," the guy began anew, "David Mittleman."

"Finally, he got my name right. And then, after I was on for about twenty minutes, the guy who booked me came over and said the sound system is shot, you don't have to do the rest of your act. It was," Steve jokes, "like getting paroled."

Not a red-letter night. But there was at least one thing good about that show—nobody heckled him. He hasn't always been so lucky. There was, for example, the time he was headlining in Toledo, and his brother and sister-in-law drove all the way from Buffalo to catch his act for the first time. Naturally he was nervous but when he heard some guy mercilessly heckle the opening act, he was really in a sweat.

His worries weren't groundless. There he was, standing on stage, lights in his eyes, unable to see anyone in the audience, and this same guy on the left started in. Steve reports that "I put him

away a few times." The jerk, however, was dauntless. During a bit about the National Rifle Association, he even went so far as yelling "Shoot the niggers."

"My mouth," says Mittleman, "dropped. I'm in shock and then all of a sudden this guy on the right yells, 'Shoot the kikes.' Well, I totally go into this whole thing about 'How can you people say these things?' I really lay into them. It was terrible. I cut my set short because I couldn't regain the momentum."

Afterwards, as he watched policemen escort the first heckler from the club, a group of college students wearing yarmulkes stopped by to apologize for yelling something out during his show. What was that? Mittleman wondered. "We didn't say 'Shoot the kikes,'" one of them informed him. "We said, 'Shoot that guy.'"

Oops. Hey, these things happen. Everybody's ears play little tricks on them now and again. But there was no mistaking the anti-Semitism another time, during a show in Ocean City, Maryland. Mittleman walked on stage and "before I said a word this guy screamed out, 'You look Jewish!'" Steve returned the volley with "probably the best response I ever had to something like that." Without missing a beat, he said, "You look prejudiced."

steve mittleman

"A lot of times," Mittleman reports, "hecklers walk up to you after they've destroyed your act and say, 'I hope I helped you out.' It's sort of a self-justification—as if they're being charitable." And Steve knows this all too well. That was exactly what a guy in Fresno said to him as cops removed the drunken buttinsky from the club. "It was," Mittleman says, "the saddest thing I ever saw."

But almost as sad was that time when several inanimate objects interrupted him during a show at a New York City college. Only half the chairs in the room faced the stage and the stage faced four elevators. "I followed a guy who sang the

saddest folk songs of all time," he says, laughing, "and the elevators never open during one of his songs. But I go up and every ten seconds, they're opening. 'Hi, nice to be here.' Ding. 'How ya doin?' Ding.

"A human being I can deal with," he concludes, "but being heckled by four elevators. . . . "

STEVE ON. . . .

Foreign cuisine: The French invented escargot—eating snails. Who came up with this? Who are the first people to come up with this? A really poor French family? A bunch of unexpected guests drop by, nothing in the house and the wife says, 'Be right back—I'll see what I can dig up in the yard'?

His elders: I'm not saying my grandmother's old but she has real teeth and a false head.

Holiday memories: I grew up in a very Jewish family. We didn't celebrate Christmas season; we celebrated tax season. Every year my father would take me to sit on an accountant's lap and I'd ask for deductions.

'I grew up in a very Jewish family. We didn't celebrate Christmas season; we celebrated tax season.'

Robert Wuhl, that one failed television pilot aside ("It was called 'Sniff' and it stunk") has done pretty well for himself. You see, in addition to his stand-up career, the New Jersey native has garnered feature roles in such movies as *Hollywood Knights*, *Bull Durham*, *Good Morning, Vietnam* and *Batman* and starring roles in *Missing Pieces* and *The Mistress*. And, along the way, he has worked with some real heavy hitters—people like Kevin Costner, Robin Williams and, the guy he says he was most impressed by, Jack Nicholson.

"He is the coolest son of a bitch on the face of the earth," says Wuhl with a grin. "I'll tell you how cool he is. We were at a party and this girl came up and said, 'Would you like to dance?' And he said, 'Wrong verb.'"

Yes, extremely cool.

But there are other stars he thinks are rather cool, as well: stars like Billy Crystal, the aforementioned Costner, Lea Thompson, and Marlee Matlin. Cool stars who all made cameo appearances on his 1990 HBO special, "Robert Wuhl's World Tour," which was shot in one night in one city (it was all part of the joke, folks). And, despite the fact that only Matlin had something nice to say about him in her pre-taped "heartfelt testimonial" (Costner and Crystal called Wuhl an asshole and Thompson one-upped them by insisting that he was a dick), Wuhl still thought it was cool.

"And the best part of it all is they all worked for scale." Then, after a short pause, he concludes. "A bathroom scale."

Finally, in addition to all the movies and the specials, Robert also got to help Billy Crystal write the material he used when he hosted the Grammys (in '88 and '89) and the Oscars (in '90 and '91). While Wuhl had a great time at all of those affairs, he was especially tickled to be at the Grammys the year that Prince showed up with a pack of bodyguards.

"It's important to have bodyguards at the Grammys," Wuhl points out, "because you never know when John Denver is going to snap."

ROBERT ON. . . .

Cartoon questions: What about the curious relationship between Popeye and Bluto? What do we really know about these two men?

They've both been on the boat a long time. And when they get off, they compete for the affection of Olive Oyl—who just might be the ugliest woman ever created. They're fighting over a girl with an Adam's apple. . . .

And what do we know about Ms. Oyl? We know that she has an illegitimate baby named Swee' Pea. Now, where did he come from? Who is the father?

Wimpy? Wim-pea? Obviously, he was getting more than hamburgers on Tuesdays.

Yoko Ono's singing voice: If it was a fight, they'd stop it.

Tough questions: How come dogs never step in shit? And they have twice as many chances.

Things that are hard to swallow: Baby, my dick is so big it has a knee in it!

Musical preferences: I like rap music. My favorite group is an all-female group, Run-PMS.

robert wuhl

'If Yoko Ono's singing voice was a fight, they'd stop it.'

Wait till you hear this. Will Durst's career started after he had a little chat with Ronald McDonald. We're serious. You can't make this stuff up, folks.

It was in November of 1974, Will was living in his native Milwaukee writing a humor column for a local underground newspaper, and studying theater at the University of Wisconsin. It was okay, but he just wasn't getting very many parts and he was really aching to get onto a stage so. . . .

"The local Ronald McDonald—the guy who created the part of Ronald McDonald," says Durst (beginning what proves to be a long explanation), "whose name was Alexi Jankowski—he changed his name to Aye Jaye—he came from a circus family so he knew about clowning. . . .

"Anyhow," he continues (after quickly running through Alexi's credentials as well as the story of his McDonald's audition), "he had been a stand-up comic, and I had met him and told him I wanted to be a stand-up too. Well, there was a revue at the airport, kind of a lounge revue with singers and Broadway songs and they had a comic in a tuxedo—the whole deal. So the comic was leaving the show and Ronald—er, Aye Jaye—told me there was an audition.

"So I put together a five-minute set using all the funny parts of my humor columns, and I went on stage and I died. *I died!*"

Well Ronald—er, Aye Jaye—never said it was going to be Mc-easy. But two nights later, things starting getting better when Will tried it again, this time at a place without a runway nearby. "I was pretty good," he remembers. "So I started doing it every Monday night."

Through the years his schedule has definitely become more demanding. There are the club dates across the country, the TV work, and a bi-weekly column for the *San Francisco Examiner*. "I just try to make people laugh out loud on purpose," he says. And, as if all that wasn't enough to keep him busy, there was a short-lived political career a few years back.

It was a chance, Will figured, to walk a mile in the other guy's shoes. He had been making fun of government officials for years (i.e., "George Bush is everything you always wanted in the Reagan administration and less—he's like Reagan Lite"), so he reasoned that the least he could do was give it a try himself. So in 1987, armed with a catchy slogan ("Vote For Durst—or Don't"), and not much else, he ran for mayor of San Francisco.

"It basically started as a publicity stunt," Will admits, "but then I got caught up in it."

With a total investment of $1,200—$800 for the candidate's filing fee and $400 for bumperstickers and buttons—Durst hit the campaign trail. His drive for office, however, lost much of its appeal along the way. Despite the fact that he finished the race "even more cynical about politics because it's all about money," he felt he was doing a disservice to the voters.

Still, his $1,200 outlay yielded him some 1,900 votes. And that, he points out, isn't bad considering that the winner of the race spent "over a million dollars" for approximately 650,000 votes.

"So," he jokes, "on a dollar-per-vote basis, I *am* the mayor of San Francisco."

WILL ON. . . .

George Bush: His role model isn't Ronald Reagan. It's Thurston P. Howell III. I kept expecting him to start his inauguration speech with '*Lovey!*'

Dan Quayle: He's as vacant as a Houston high-rise and he's just a chicken bone away from the presidency. Let's hope Babs knows the Heimlich maneuver. . . . When he was asked what he would do if he became president, he said, 'I'd

will durst

say a little prayer.' Yeah—him and 245 million other Americans! I don't know if the earth could survive the seismic shock of all those knees hitting the ground at the same time.

Ronald Reagan: Most presidents are figureheads. Reagan was a hood ornament. But no matter what you thought of his policies, you had to admire his ability not to get involved in them.

Mario Cuomo: He'd never get elected president. To people in the Midwest, Mario isn't the name of the chief executive, Mario is the guy who runs the Tilt-a-Whirl at the carnival.

Politicians who lump drugs together: You can't do that. Crack is to pot what an Uzi is to a banana.

'Dan Quayle is as vacant as a Houston high-rise and he's just a chicken bone away from the presidency. Let's hope Babs knows the Heimlich maneuver.'

Foreign policy: We just signed a new trade agreement with the Japanese. We agreed to bend over and they agreed not to distribute the negatives.

Togetherness: Everyone's excited by the reunified Germany, especially the French. They're already planting trees along their boulevards so the next invading German army can march in the shade.

Even from the beginning, Brett Butler's monikers alone spelled something special. Born Brett Ashley Anderson, she was named for the heroine of *The Sun Also Rises*. Six years later, when her divorced mother remarried, her last name was changed to Butler.

But her childhood in the South definitely belied the lyricism of her names. Still, the woman who jokes that "it's a miracle that I don't have four kids, a bloody nose, and live in a trailer park in Tallapoosa," doesn't want her life to be chronicled like some "oh, poor me" melodrama. It happened, she figures, it's over, life goes on. "Listen," says Brett, sidestepping some of the more personal details, "if I had had a normal childhood, I probably wouldn't be a comedian."

At least not *her* kind of comedian, to be sure. Below the pretty brunette's light southern drawl, you see, lurk some pretty dark memories—memories that have a habit of finding their way into her act.

Main among these are the horrors she endured courtesy of her first husband, a Macon, Georgia "redneck," whom she met and married just shy of her twentieth birthday. Their small wedding, Brett points out with an ironic laugh, took place on the same day that Prince Charles of England took Lady Diana Spencer's hand in marriage. In retrospect, it was a date that was not entirely (despite what the British tabloids believed) a good day for happy endings.

"The day after we got married," Butler recalls of her ex-husband, "he hit me."

That proved to be only the first of many times that she felt the physical sting of his disapproval. The beatings continued—even sending her to hospitals and women's shelters "three or four times"—until one day he was asleep on the couch and a distraught Butler contemplated "splitting his face open with a pipe wrench."

She quickly decided to pass on that urge. Instead, she packed what she could in a couple of bags and left for good, eventually landing in Texas. "I left him with everything," she says, and then adds with a weak smile, "but then we didn't have much."

That first year was a tough one, but at the end of it she finally screwed up enough courage to climb onto a stage. "I started doing comedy in women's shelters on weekends," says Butler, who is now happily married to a New York lawyer ("the antithesis of my first husband"). "It doesn't seem like it, but it's a good place to begin. Your audience has a bloody nose, no money, and two kids—and she's laughing! You figure, 'I've gotta be good.'"

And in the nearly ten years since she first started, Brett has gotten better at her craft and hopes to fashion a one-woman show from her material. But even more important, Butler insists that she has gotten past her personal anger and she now channels her energies into working for assorted political and social causes. Among other things, she has organized anti-apartheid benefits, marched on Washington in a pro-choice rally, and performed at charity functions in support of everything from women's shelters to organizations that provide meals for elderly shut-ins.

Still, a definite by-product of that anger has honed one of the sharpest edges in comedy today and it will, no doubt, always be a tangible element in Butler's wonderfully provocative act. "After all," she declares, "I've had too much happen to me in my life to be trite."

Talk about your understatements.

BRETT ON. . . .

Her first marriage: I was so young when I got married, I thought a battered wife was the kind you dipped in bread crumbs and deep-fried.

Her birthplace: I'm going to write a book about the South. I'm going to call it, *When Beautiful Places Happen to Bad People*.

brett butler

Aging graciously: The older I get, the simpler the definition of maturity seems: It is the lengthening of time between when I realize someone is a jackass and when I tell them that they're one. Maybe that's why there's four years between elections.

Politics: There wouldn't be a big deal to see a female president. Maybe they'd start calling it the 'Ova Office.'

The rag: I would like it if men had to partake in the same hormonal cycles to which we're subjected monthly. Maybe that's why men declare war—because they have a need to bleed on a regular basis.

> *'I would like it if men had to partake in the same hormonal cycles to which we're subjected monthly. Maybe that's why men declare war—because they have a need to bleed on a regular basis.'*

Richard Lewis had performed a great set at the "Comic Relief '90" benefit at Radio City Music Hall and now, a few hours later at a huge party at a hotel ballroom, he just wanted to relax over a glass of wine and chat with a couple of friends. Instead, he was on the run—he had to be. Every time he tried to stop, large groups of seemingly rabid fans would surround him, demanding autographs, handshakes, or a few minutes of his time. At first it was fun, but he was exhausted and this particular exercise became real tired, real quick.

"I've got to get out of here," he finally declared to his publicist, throwing his hands in the air and shaking his head. And then he smiled wryly, adding as he got closer to the door, "I can't believe this. It's amazing—all of a sudden I'm like Elvis."

It's not that Richard Lewis means to complain, it's just that if he didn't he would run the risk of ruining his career. Besides, after more than twenty-odd years on the stand-up stage, he's gotten really damn good at it. He is, if you will, the King of Kvetching. So what makes Richard run at the mouth?

"Approval from my family was a major source of why I went into comedy," he insists. But instead of getting their approval, he says that "It was sort of a stupid way to go because I got the reverse—I got rejected."

As proof, take the episode that he was forced to live through while filming *The Wrong Guys*, a poorly received 1988 adventure-comedy that featured Lewis as well as Louie Anderson, Richard Belzer, and Franklin Ajaye. "In the movie," he remembers, "my real mother plays my mother. It was like a Freudian dream come true. And she was absolutely thrilled to be in it. But when she found that she could buy her wardrobe for half price, well, that was it!

"Now at the end of the movie, we're drowning in this mud hole, and our mothers show up and are supposed to save us. Notice I say 'supposed' to save us," he stresses. "I'm in this mud, I reach out for her sleeve and *she pulls back!* I couldn't believe it. 'Don't touch me,' she says, 'I'm buying this outfit.'"

For anybody else, this would have caused a discussion at the family dinner table. For Richard, however, it's good for a five-minute bit—at least. And when he gets started on one of his comic tirades, he takes no prisoners—whether it's his mother, other family members, or his ex-girlfriends. He also takes his time. The man is best described as a careening, uncontrollable train travelling from New York to Los Angeles by way of Phoenix, Anchorage, New Orleans, and Chicago. He'll get there, but he's got to pick up all of his emotional baggage first.

Still, he insists, comedy isn't his way of getting even. "I just can't lie on stage. I've gotten into trouble but whatever strengths I have as a comedian, I think honesty is one of them. I think it's cathartic. And five out of the six friends I've had have said it was cathartic too. "The one who didn't," he jokes, "I blew off."

Obviously, *that* one was not his mother, even though he's blamed her for nearly every neurosis he's developed ("Her Yiddish name," says Richard, "is I'm *tawwwwking* to you!"). But his mother, he says, "is no problem at all" these days.

"She lives to be mocked," says Lewis, a veteran of more than 45 "Late Night" appearances. "She tells me, 'Please ridicule me on "Letterman."'"

He always does. Such a good son.

RICHARD ON. . . .

How he gets through the day: I have problems flown in fresh daily wherever I am.

Women who want to get too close: I'm sorry. I can't have sex and get intimate at the same time.

His parents: They meant well. They read all

richard lewis

these books. Their favorite one was *Spare the Joy*.

Family outings: I went to a play with my family. We went to see *Les Misèrables*. I thought it was gonna be like a play about one of my family's Seders.

His ancestors: My grandfather had delusions of other people's grandeur.

Holidays: They should be a blessing. But usually in the Lewis family, on New Year's Eve we'd sit around and watch our hopes drop.

The old homestead: It's like the Suffer Dome. It's the House that Guilt built . . . . When I was growing up I kept my door open so I could get cross humiliation from my brother and sister.

Masturbation: I don't masturbate unless I promise myself that afterwards I'll take myself out to dinner and a show.

'My family's house was like the Suffer Dome. It's the House that Guilt built . . . . When I was growing up I kept my door open so I could get cross humiliation from my brother and sister.'

"**G**etting shot," says Rick Aviles, a tad too nonchalantly, "is really no big deal."

Aviles should know considering that he's been on both sides of that situation. In the 1990 blockbuster *Ghost*, he shot and killed Patrick Swayze. In *The Godfather Part III*, Aviles was the guy who bought the farm after he broke into Andy Garcia's on-screen apartment. Garcia, so you'll know, did the honors—and much more.

"At one point," Aviles remembers, "[Garcia] thought he was helping me out, trying to help me get into character. So he put this empty gun near my nose and got into my face, and he said, 'You don't know if it has bullets or not!'

"Like he was trying to be tough with me," continues Aviles, who adds with a little laugh, "I wanted to smack that gun right out of his hand. He didn't know who he was dealing with."

Apparently not. Rick Aviles, you see, knows from tough. The oldest of four children of working class Puerto Rican parents ("You're in the middle," he says of his heritage on stage, "you're not black, you're not white—you're *here*"), Rick was raised in a public housing project on Manhattan's Lower East Side. It was the kind of neighborhood where the Brady Bunch wouldn't have been found dead (then again, it's exactly where they *would* have been found dead). It was a place where the parks were covered with cement, and the streets were littered with stripped cars and tough kids with too much time on their hands and too little honest money in their pockets.

Rick was one of those kids, and he eventually developed "a little problem with the druggies," which, in turn, led to even more problems with the law. A fair number of arrests resulted in a couple of all-expenses paid vacations in stir. "I was never in prison," he says stressing that last word, "but, yeah, I did some time in, like, county jails and stuff."

Finally, in the early '80s, he made his way to Boston where his mother had relocated. Once there, he worked as a printer, and then he started doing comedy in a park. On his first day of performance, he made five dollars and quit his day job—a move that he didn't find all that odd.

"I always made money on the street," he says. "When I was a kid I shined shoes, sold papers. . . . Comedy was just another way to make money. I never saw it as an art form that you had to work at."

By the time he returned to New York, the rubber-faced comic was an old hand at street performance and earned a living by (among other devices) mimicking tourists. "When I'd pass the hat," he says, "there would be yen in there and francs and marks and whatever." There were also old-fashioned American coins—so many, he jokes, that "I always had change for the laundry."

rick aviles

In the mid-'80s he finally got off the street and started taking comedy seriously. (And not so coincidentally, he stopped doing drugs on January 3rd, 1985.) A couple of years later he began to feel accepted by his peers and these days, he says, "I'm starting to feel like a comedian—I know I can say shit and make it funny."

Certain personal topics, however, remain taboo. Though he jokes on stage that he "experimented with drugs once or twice—*for about fifteen years*," he says that there are things he just doesn't want to talk about. "There are parts of my life," he says, "that just aren't funny. Some of it is pretty painful."

Still, when the question is broached he just can't resist the crack. What exactly has he done that he would never recount on stage? "Well," he says with a hearty laugh, "just that time I blew the guy in jail." Makes sense to us.

RICK ON. . . .

The fundamentals of reading: We're six years old and the first book they give us is 'Dick and Jane.'

'Jane saw Dick. Jane liked Dick. Jane played with Dick.'

I closed the book, I played hooky and I went looking for Jane.

His hometown: Most New Yorkers have an attitude—even the winos. 'Hey! Gimme some money you piece of shit!'

Shopping with girlfriends: All of a sudden, they make you their fashion consultant. 'Does this make me look fat?'

'No, it doesn't make you look fat—you already are fat. I love you anyway, but baby, you're a whale.'

Pushy salespeople: Every city I go to, a different ethnic group tries to sell me smoke . . . . Did you ever see Jewish marijuana dealers? 'Vat do you mean it's not an ounce? That's an ounce! I been in the business twenty years!'

> *When we're six years old and the first book they give us to read is Dick and Jane. "Jane saw Dick. Jane liked Dick. Jane played with Dick." I closed the book, I played hooky, and I went looking for Jane.*

Even if you don't get what Barry Sobel is talking about, you have to appreciate his apparently endless supply of energy. The patter, you see, heavily sprinkled with references to pop culture, is non-stop and delivered in seemingly random order.

For instance, his riff on stupid movie ideas ("Sylvester Stallone as the greatest miniature golfer ever!" Sobel chants, hands thrown above his head in perfect "Rocky" pose, "Windmill! . . . Arnold Schwarzenegger is mad—about *Bingo!* 'I'll get I-19 and then you'll be in trouble!'") might lead right into being a roadie for the Village People, ("Indian, pick up those feathers, there are only 15 minutes to get on the bus!" "Wait. All the musical equipment is in Florida and we're in New York City? Where am I going to get eight tambourines by nine o'clock?" "Boot, boots, boots, boots, boots, boots, mocassions, boots, boots. All right, everyone on the bus, let's go!") and all without benefit of a verbal bridge.

barry sobel

"Silly audience," Sobel has been known to instruct them, "segues are for kids."

They could be useful, however. For example, after a particularly frenetic performance at Caroline's some years ago, one middle-aged man opined that, "He was great. I didn't understand half of what he said, but he was terrific." That kind of thing happens all the time. In fact, *Robocop* star Peter Weller might have said it best after he first saw Sobel perform at Los Angeles's Improv club in the mid-'80s.

"I had just finished my set," remembers the guy who was a featured player on TV's "227," "and I got an okay response from the crowd. So, I was walking out and this guy, Peter Weller, runs out of the place to tell me—now I'm kinda paraphrasing here, it was actually much more dramatic the way he said it—that my act was like

this compelling journey through time and space. That I go all over the place and I compel people to come along with me."

And some of the people who have gone along for that ride comprise a rather stellar list. Tom Hanks declared himself a fan and then hired Sobel to write material with Hanks and to coach him for his turn as a stand-up in the movie *Punchline* (he, Sobel, and Weller still take in L.A. Kings hockey games together). Eddie Murphy saw and so liked Sobel, who kids that his "jokes aren't for everybody—just the sexy people," that he put the comic in one of his HBO specials. River Phoenix, says Sobel, was "very complimentary"—as were Johnny Depp and Richard Pryor. Ditto for music's M.C. Hammer—who even mixed a couple of rap tunes for the Brooklyn boy.

The list goes on. But as Sobel himself might say, à la many rock and roll singers, "I can't do no more—I can't go on!" But he does. He always does.

"I've always remained a kid," says the guy who cherishes the moment that he met "and bummed a cigarette" from Madonna. "I'm still not jaded about meeting famous people. I still think that's a fun aspect of this job.

"As a stand-up comedian," he continues, "you get kicked in the face by club owners who want to tell you what jokes to do; by bookers who hate you and won't hire you; by drunks who yell at you. To have a Pryor or a Hanks tell you that they like what you do, it just makes it all worth it."

The only thing better than that, he says, is the feeling he had after doing his first three "Tonight Show" spots. "I did panel all three times," he says excitedly. "So each time I was doing comedy with Johnny Carson. It's like you're a guitar player and you get to jam with Springsteen in front of everyone. There's nothing more euphoric than that."

Sobel's beginnings, it should be noted, were decidedly less glamorous. He grew up in Bor-

ough Park, Brooklyn, the son of a printer father and a mother who "worked as a receptionist in a medical place." He won't say when he was born or how old he is at the moment ("I don't know dates," he jokes, "and even if I did, I'd lie") but he will say that he left home at seventeen and headed to San Francisco where he "moved in with my hip—meaning they smoked pot—cousins and started going to college."

"I," he declares with a chuckle, "like John Travolta in *Saturday Night Fever,* just had to get out of Brooklyn."

Within moments of his arrival in 'Frisco, apparently, Sobel, who has been jokingly introduced "as the hardest working white man in show business," went to see an improvisation group perform and having already downed a total of one beer ("I was pretty wild," he insists), took up the group's offers to be an on-stage volunteer. "I went up," he remembers, "and I liked it."

So much so, in fact, that he left school and started doing comedy full-time. Then, after a couple of years in northern California, Sobel moved south to Los Angeles "where," he overstates dramatically, "I've been suffering ever since—serving the perennial actor/comedian death sentence until I become rich and famous enough to move somewhere else."

BARRY ON. . . .
Popular Culture:
I'm not the Beastie Boys / or Run-DMC /
I'm not Jay Leno / Or someone named Shecky /
I'm just the motherfuckin' king of jokes /
There is none more funny / If this was Las Vegas /
You'd be throwin' down money /
See here I am / So understand /
That when I kick it up live / I'm in the promised land /

I'm a stand-up comic / Well that's my line / And I'd like to know your zodiac / Z-z-z-zodiac / Z-z-z-zodiac / Z-z-z-zodiac/ Z-z-z-zodiac sign.

Y'see, the only problem I got in my mind / I'm a comedian, right
but I can only remember the PUNCHLINE!
Ping pong balls? I thought you said King Kong's balls! / Disaster?! Lady, it killed her! / Would I? Peg leg! / Oh no! Now all the fish are gonna smell like that / Hey, I don't want no damn pancakes / Jesus, y'gonna play golf or y'gonna fool around? / How do y'*think* I got this nifty cross? / Peter, I can see your house from here / Can you put me up for the night? / They both eat rice / Shredded wheat! / Need another seven astronauts / I asked for a *Bud* Light / What does this button do? / Fuck the mailman. Give him five bucks, breakfast was my idea / This Chinese guy . . . we were lookin' all over the mine for him . . . this Chinese guy comes out of nowhere and goes, 'SUPLISE! Suplise!' / Then Cleopatra goes, 'Not now, I'm on my pyramid' / Little Red Riding Hood turns to the Wolf and goes, 'You're gonna eat me like it says in the book' / These are jokes . . . These are *all* the jokes . . . BOIINNG! Silly audience, segues are for kids.

> *Imagine what it would be like being a roadie for the Village People: "Indian, pick up those feathers, there are only 15 minutes to get on the bus!"*

Steven Wright has a much different way of thinking about things than the rest of us—not that there's something wrong with that. In fact, it's quite all Wright. Take, for instance, this comic observation: "I hate when my foot falls asleep during the day—that means it's going to be up all night." Or, this one: "There's a fine line between fishing and just standing on the shore like an idiot." Or, finally, this skeptical speculation: "My theory of evolution? I think Darwin was adopted."

It is a rather odd perspective to say the least. And when Steven gives voice to these extraordinary observations via his trademark deadpan delivery, the gangly comic with the halo of bushy hair can seem downright surrealistic. It is the kind of outlook that would definitely worry most parents. His, however, didn't seem to notice.

"They didn't know I was like this," Wright says, shaking his head and laughing. "They didn't know. I was just saying this stuff to my friends when I was out of the house. When I'd come home it was just, 'Pass the potatoes.' They didn't know until I was on stage.

"But then I didn't even know I was this twisted until I started doing my act—until I started sitting down and going, 'All right, I have to write a bunch of stuff here.' And it's just focusing all of this madness into a few minutes. And then, it looks like you're really crazy."

But, to prove that he's really no weirder than the next guy, he explains that "my act is an hour long, and if I said that hour's work of material over the course of a year in conversation—two jokes here or two jokes there—you wouldn't think anything was wrong. But if you come to see that hour in one sitting, you leave thinking, 'This guy's out of his mind.'"

Not so for everyone. Some, like Peter LaSalle, a producer for "The Tonight Show," thought he was just out of this world. LaSalle was in Boston checking out colleges with his teenage son when he wandered into a comedy club and caught newcomer Wright's act. Three weeks later—without benefit of a manager, an agent or any previous television exposure—Wright made his debut on that venerable late night program.

"It was amazing," Steven remembers, "to go from that club to 'The Tonight Show.' The studio audience had 500 people, which was the biggest audience I ever played. Even if I hadn't gone on television," he points out, "it was still my biggest audience."

To make things even better, Carson so liked what he saw on that Friday night that Wright was invited back to do the show the following Thursday. "Everything changed immediately," he says of his career. "It was like a car accident—the next thing I knew it was over."

In truth, it had only just begun. Concerts, HBO specials, movies (*Desperately Seeking Susan*)—even an Oscar (for his short film, *The Appointments of Dennis Jennings*)—followed. And also, so did the crowds. Good thing, too.

"I remember telling my mother some of my new material," Steven says, "and she looked at me, not like I was crazy, but like she wasn't paying attention. So I made her listen and she didn't like it. She said, 'That's not funny. Lucille Ball is funny.'

"But then she'd come to the club and she'd be laughing during the show," he continues. "And the next time I was home, I said, 'Mom, why were you laughing at the show but you weren't laughing in the kitchen?' And she said, 'Oh, shut the hell up.'

"People have to be in the environment," he concludes. "That's why I don't try my stuff out on anyone, one on one. If I do, they just look at me like they're pushing the button under the table for the silent alarm."

steven wright

STEVEN ON. . . .

Arriving in this world: When I was a baby, I kept a diary. Day one: Still tired from the move. Day two: Everyone talks to me like I'm an idiot.

Firearm etiquette: If you shoot a mime, should you use a silencer?

Leisure activity: Once I went fishing with Salvador Dali. He was using a dotted line. He caught every other fish.

Inquiring minds: I walked up to a tourist information booth and said, 'Tell me about some people who were here last year.'

Science and nature: Sponges grow in the ocean. That kills me. I wonder how much deeper the ocean would be if that didn't happen?

His alma mater: My school colors were clear. 'I'm not naked—I'm in the band.'

> *'Once I went fishing with Salvador Dali. He was using a dotted line. He caught every other fish.'*

Logic: Whenever I fill out an application and it says, 'In case of emergency, notify . . . ,' I put 'doctor.' What the hell is my mother going to do?

Predestination: I was lying in bed with my girlfriend the other night and she said, 'If you could know how and when you were going to die, would you want to know?' I said, 'No.' She said, 'Forget it, then.'

Emo Philips was born in Downers Grove, Illinois, and he lived there until he was eight years old when his parents moved to another town. When he was twelve, he says, he found them. Still, the lanky coleslaw connoisseur insists, he was the product of a somewhat loving home.

"When I was a child," Emo recalls, "I couldn't wait for the first snowfall. I would run to the door and yell. 'Let me in! Let me in!' You know the deal."

And it was inside that modest house where the guy who came in from the cold developed his sartorial tastes. His mother, apparently, was his biggest influence.

"Once I was going out," says Judy Tenuta's husband running a hand through his blunt-cut mane, "and my Mom didn't like the pants I was wearing. She kept telling me, 'Put on your grandfather's good pants. Put on your grandfather's good pants.' I finally decided she was right, so I got out the shovel . . ."

And he must have worn those, as he does all his other second-hand duds, with such flair! The day we meet, in fact, his ensemble is almost color coordinated. The light blue crew-neck shirt he picked up at a Salvation Army store is accented by brown, white, and dark blue stripes. The light blue in the shirt is a near match for the blue background of the resale store pants. What's more, the nautical stencils on the pants actually match the stripe colors on the shirt. The lace-up shoes and belt, in the meantime, are black—kind of a neutral choice—and the socks, one black, the other brown, sort of pull the whole thing together.

All of which surprises the six-foot-two-inch, 145 pound comic to no end. "Ironically," he insists, pulling hard at his knit shirt. "I've never been much of a fashion hound. In fact, even when I'm naked I clash with myself."

Of course, whether Emo chooses his clothes because he likes them or because they fit into his act is anyone's guess. He's a Buster Keaton fan, you see, and he refuses to come out of character. Even in one-on-one conversation, even on New York's ultra-chic Fifth Avenue, and even at the threshold of the incredibly pricey Trump Tower ("There's a Taco Bell in here, isn't there?" he deadpans upon entering the pink marble structure). Whatever the case may be, however, he seems genuinely happy with his, shall we say, eclectic wardrobe. Still, marching to the beat of your own fashion drummer can sometimes prove an emotionally rocky existence.

"I once went out with this girl," he's reminded as he passes a swank haberdashery, "and she said, 'Emo, I'm ashamed to be seen with you because of the way you dress.' I said, 'Okay, you can dress me any way you want.' So she takes me to this fancy men's shop and puts me in this $500 suit and afterwards she said, 'Emo, I owe you an apology. I really thought it was the clothing.'"

Further proof that the world has always been wrong. It seems nice clothes don't necessarily make the man. Sometimes all it takes are some used pants.

EMO ON. . . .

Women: You can't live with them and you can't get them to dress up in skimpy, little Nazi costumes.

His ex-girlfriend: She was very sexy. She reminded me of the Sphinx because she was very mysterious and eternal and solid . . . and her nose was shot off by French soldiers.

Heartbreak: I caught my girlfriend in bed with another guy. I was crushed. I said, 'Get off me, you two.'

Cocktail conversation: People always ask me, 'Where were you when Kennedy was shot?' Well, I don't have an alibi.

emo philips

Life: Probably the toughest time in anyone's life is when you have to murder a loved one because they are the Devil. Other than that, it's been a good day.

Exercise: I ran three miles today. Finally I said, 'Okay, lady, take back your purse.'

Private pleasure: Oh, yes, I've tried my hand at sex.

Dating: Back in high school, my buddies tried to put the make on anything that moved. I told them, 'Why limit yourselves?'

Faith: When I was a kid I used to pray every night for a new bicycle. Then I realized that the Lord, in his wisdom, didn't work that way. So I just stole one and asked him to forgive me.

'When I was a kid I used to pray every night for a new bicycle. Then I realized that the Lord, in his wisdom, didn't work that way. So I just stole one and asked him to forgive me.'

Robert Klein set the pace for a generation of comics. While it seems that he patterned his confident stage manner and pleasant demeanor from elder joke tellers like Bob Hope and Johnny Carson, this child of the '50s brought something that was rare in the world of comedy when he arrived on the laugh scene in the mid-'60s: he had a sharp, socially aware Lenny Bruce-like edge that cut through his work.

Take, for instance, Klein's now-classic bit that skewers anti-Semitism by dealing with his fantasy of ordering a kosher meal on a plane only to be totally intimidated by an announcement over the loud speaker ("Will the *Jew* who ordered the kosher meal please make himself known? Will the *Jew*. . . .") And jokes like that also pointed to something else that was new in comedy—gone was the traditional set-up/pay-off style that was so common. In its place he introduced a stream-of-consciousness delivery that would open the door for the more manic likes of Robin Williams, Richard Belzer, and Barry Sobel, and others yet to come.

robert klein

Even if Robert Klein didn't know he was such a trendsetter when he started out, he did know that he was participating in a respectable art form. "Standing in one spot," he once said, "and making people laugh is a unique calling." And, he figures, it's a solo sport in which hecklers are neither amusing nor tolerated. "I have a kind of hang-up about the dignity in what I do," Robert said in another interview. "Making people laugh, I've come to think, is a damned noble pursuit."

Especially the way he does it. Klein never goes for the cheap shot—there's no funny filth in his repertoire, no string of four-letter words, no tasteless send-ups. He's also no Pollyanna—isolated curses find their way into his act, but, as he points out, "They are part of adult conversation and I use them properly." And he surrounds them with funny assessments of the ironies we encounter in everyday life.

For example, take this years-old bit that lampoons law firms such as Jacoby and Meyers that set up offices in places like Sears stores. "You get the lawnmower, Ma," Klein says, exaggerating the last word with an Appalachian-ish twang. "I'll check on the murder conviction and then meet you in garden supplies."

He can even make the most horrible topics—i.e., AIDS—funny without making an audience wince. Take, for instance, the title track of his 1990 album, "Let's Not Make Love" (A Love Song For the 90s), which was inspired by a chance encounter a few years back.

The by-then divorced Klein was at a party when a comely young thing approached him. "This woman," he says, "hit on me. And as if to put her best sexual foot forward, she said, 'Don't worry about me, I'm tested twice a year. I give blood.'"

When Klein (who was nominated for a Tony Award for his turn in the musical *They're Playing Our Song*) finally stopped laughing, he started writing. And the resulting tune goes, in part: "You look at me / I look at you / Looking at each others' all we're gonna do / Read the papers, watch TV / And I'm sure that you'll agree / Let's not make love."

And that's not the only bit of wisdom he has given people over the years. Many younger comics have sought out his advice and, like his act, it was always right on target.

"I went to see him at a small club in Philadelphia," says comic Wayne Cotter, "and I went backstage after the show and told him that I wanted to be a comedian and asked him what I should do.

"He told me, 'Perform in front of people,'" remembers Cotter. He adds with a little laugh, "I thought it was really good advice."

ROBERT ON. . . .

Extraterrestrials: Why are there never very credible accounts of aliens from outer space? Why is it that flying saucers always land in the backyard of some Ozark moron who just drank Sunoco 260 with his brother? If they want to contact us, why don't they land in Carl Sagan's backyard or the Princeton School for Advanced Studies? Or Mike Wallace's back yard from '60 Minutes'? If he put a microphone in their face, they'd go back to outer space in a second. Mike: 'In other words, you little green bastards are frauds?"

Charity: The proceeds from tonight's show are going to the Kurt Waldheim Fund. We're sending Kurt to the Harry Lorraine Memory Institute to try to remember five years of his life. It's terrible, the poor guy forgot. 'It vas 1941, I vas in Vienna, I vas drinking a cup of *café mit sclage*, suddenly it vas *1946!*'

> **‘I'm sure George Washington, the father of our country, would be proud to know that we celebrate his birthday every year with a mattress sale.’**

Disrespect: I'm sure George Washington, the father of our country, would be proud to know that we celebrate his birthday every year with a mattress sale.

Outlandish advertisements: I saw one that said, 'Ninety-nine out of a hundred people prefer the Dodge 600 ES to the Mercedes Benz.' I'd like to meet these people. I'd like to give them a Rorschach test. What do they use, North Korean Police torture electric schock methods to get those results?

'Which do you prefer, the Dodge or the Mercedes?'

'The Mercedes.' (Shock) 'The Dodge! The Dodge!'

Fantasies: If I see a cigarette butt in a urinal, I aim for it. I make believe that it's some kind of Nazi installation like in *Command Decision*.

ABOUT ED EDAHL

Ed Edahl developed an interest in photography (and a sense of humor) while serving as a U.S. Army counterintelligence agent in Vietnam. He began his professional career as a newspaper photographer in Annapolis, Maryland and has worked in New York City since 1973 doing editorial, corporate, and advertising work. He started photographing comedians by taking the headliners from the original Caroline's on Eighth Avenue around the corner to his studio and shooting them with an 8 X 10 studio camera on white backgrounds, believing that more effective than stage shots. Since then, however, he has relented and shot comedians almost everywhere.

ABOUT HANK GALLO

Hank Gallo began his journalism career at the *New York Daily News* in 1978—working his way from copyboy ("two regulars, no sugar") to movie timetable clerk ("1:15, 3:15, 5:15, 7:15") to entertainment writer/editor ("It's going to be late/it better be on time"). He wrote his first story about comedians in 1984, spent much of his time chronicling the subsequent comedy boom, and enjoyed one of the most memorable assignments of his career when he spent a day with George Burns. He still finds pleasure when one of his "unknowns" becomes famous and finds it amusing that his loud, trademark staccato laugh can be heard on some of the best comedy records and TV specials.

Hank left *The News* in 1991 to work as a freelance reporter.